DIRTY DEALING

GROSSO v. MIRAMAX

WAGING WAR WITH HARVEY WEINSTEIN, AND THE SCREENPLAY THAT CHANGED HOLLYWOOD

JEFFREY ALLAN GROSSO

PERMUTED
PRESS

A PERMUTED PRESS BOOK
ISBN: 978-1-63758-297-8
ISBN (eBook): 978-1-63758-298-5

PERMUTED
PRESS
Permuted Press, LLC
New York • Nashville
permutedpress.com

Published in the United States of America
1   2   3   4   5   6   7   8   9   10

For those who dare dream. For those who aren't afraid to risk, and lose, and risk again. For those who run, and fall, and get right back up only to run faster than before. This book is for you.

And for Tricky and Trevor, who were the best of the best.

"The defining notion of any democracy is corruption."—*19th-Century Norwegian Economist Hedwig V. Klapp*

TABLE OF CONTENTS

INTRODUCTION

THE BUY-IN

IN *DIRTY DEALING: GROSSO v. MIRAMAX*, my story about waging war with Harvey Weinstein and writing the screenplay that changed Hollywood, you will find a 100 percent true story of lust, greed, betrayal, ambition, fame, power, corruption, deception, redemption, and poker. Further, you will be presented with the twisted tale of how disgraced former Miramax studio chief Harvey Weinstein, prior to his being ousted and exiled from polite society in spectacularly grotesque fashion and while still at the height of his powers, stole my screenplay, *The Shell Game*, and turned it into the mildly famous and moderately acclaimed poker movie, *Rounders*.

To put it simply, I believe that, without my *Shell Game* script, there never would have been a *Rounders* or any of the dozens of poker movies and shows that limped along in its wake. And if you'll give me half a chance, I promise that I can prove it to you well beyond any reasonable doubt. By the time all the facts are presented here, you will agree with me. Guaranteed. That is my oath to you. And that's just the beginning. What happened *after* Harvey Weinstein stole my script is actually far more amazing and unbelievable than him stealing it in the first place.

Ostensibly, this is the true tale of a crime—a theft, to be more precise. A simple theft of a screenplay, or rather, ideas, characters, settings, language, themes, and events contained in said screenplay, that turned out to not be so simple at all, and the shocking amount of chaos and consternation that said theft begat. The sturm und drang was indeed heard quite literally and loudly from coast to coast, particularly in the fancy offices, sprawling backlots, and hirsute hallways of Hollywood. This theft did not go gently into that good night. Oh, no. Far from it. It became quite the big deal, in fact, if I may paraphrase Will Ferrell in *Anchorman*.

At its heart, this is a story about corruption—of the mind, of the soul, of the courts, and of the system. Corruption of the kind that has seemingly run rampant all over our fair nation, now more than ever. Indeed, it seems like you can't turn around these days without being bombarded by an avalanche of criminal activity being perpetrated by the very same individuals and institutions that are alleged to be stalwart pillars of truth and integrity. Just tune into the daily news cycle at any given time, and you will be pummeled with wave after wave of stories about corrupt politicians, lawyers, doctors, companies, corporations, banks, financiers, and everything and everyone in between. It is literally everywhere. Upsetting as it may be, blatant, balls-out corruption seems to be the current coin of the realm. And corruption is what we will be exploring here in *Dirty Dealing*—deep-rooted, ubiquitous, sinister, all-encompassing, unrelenting corruption.

On the other side of the coin, *Dirty Dealing* is a story about perseverance, grit, determination, and luck. It is a story about poker and risk and all that implies. It's a story that isn't easy to define in a short sentence, and I don't mean that in a pompous way but rather as a testament to my tendency to digress. It is part dark comedy, part light comedy, part courtroom drama, part cautionary tale, and part memoir.

It is the story of a famous, or infamous, court battle waged against a dodgy New York City film company called Miramax that was known for helping to launch the independent film movement of the 1990s with titles such as *Pulp Fiction* and *Shakespeare in Love*. Miramax happened to have been founded and was helmed by convicted serial sexual assaulter Harvey Weinstein, who is also at the heart of this case, a case that lasted for ten long years and, in the end, forever changed not only American copyright law but also the way Hollywood itself does business.

So how did this one, seemingly innocuous screenplay, one that was written in a little beach shack in Southern California by an unknown and unsung writer who was busy playing poker for a living and banging it out in his spare time, end up having such a colossal impact on the culture at large? Well, with a little bit of luck and a decent amount of old-fashioned elbow grease, that's just one of the questions that will be answered in the following pages.

At the end of the day, after all is said and done, all I can say is that *Dirty Dealing* is a candid, honest, and 100 percent real and true story about what it means to dream and to pursue those dreams furiously and relentlessly to the very ends of the earth, no matter the cost.

CHAPTER 1

THE DECK

IN THE SUMMER OF 1995, I was living in Hermosa Beach, California and playing poker for a living. But playing poker wasn't all I was doing in those days. Whenever I wasn't at the casino, I was sequestered in the front bedroom of a small, two-bedroom, rented beach cottage that I shared with my roommate, Chopper, at 826 Manhattan Avenue, diligently writing a screenplay called *The Shell Game*.

I remember playing the CD of *Elton John's Greatest Hits* over and over and over again the entire time I was writing it, as a sort of metronomic, musical backdrop, the melodic repetition allowing me to entrance myself and stay focused on my task. Friends and random beach people would wander in and out of the shack at odd intervals and always ask why I was playing the same disc every time they entered.

"Don't touch it!" I'd yell from my workstation in the bedroom. "I need the groove…"

The story I aimed to tell was about a college student putting himself through school by playing poker, namely the specific game of Texas Hold'em. The protagonist, along with his mercurial running buddy, despite the objections of his disapproving, pretty blonde girlfriend, hangs out in the local poker clubs, plays a lot of Texas Hold'em, and eventually finds himself in hot water at the hands of a rather nasty loan shark and his crime boss employer. Now, if you are a poker player and/or fond of poker movies and this plot sounds strangely familiar to you, perhaps a bit like the 1998 Miramax release *Rounders*, starring Matt Damon and Ed Norton, then you are already up to speed.

I myself had been, just a few years prior to writing *The Shell Game* screenplay, a college kid putting himself through school by playing Texas Hold'em. My real-life running buddy and poker partner, Munchy, did actually get into some pretty serious trouble with a casino-dwelling loan shark known as the "Juice Man" and his nefarious associates. This part of the story was true. It actually happened. I felt that these real-life events were colored with a certain gritty, authentic, salacious quality that would play well on screen, so I used fictionalized versions of them in my script. That's one of the facets of this whole fiasco that was always so difficult to accept. It wasn't just that I felt they'd stolen my story; I felt that they'd stolen my life. I didn't just write it; I lived it.

In between beach volleyball games and trips to the casino for extended Hold'em sessions to support myself, it took me about six months of serious hunkering down in that bedroom to write *The Shell Game* and another few months to edit and refine it. By February of 1996, I was ready to send it out to the world. And send it out to the world I did. I dutifully printed out a dozen hard copies, as was the time, and included a one-page synopsis of the story with each script. I wrote cover letters that were custom-tailored to each recipient and consulted *The Writer's Market* reference book in the local Hermosa Beach Public Library for prospective places to mail the packages. I sent *Shell Game* scripts and letters to production companies, networks, studios, and agencies, anywhere I thought I might find a friendly ear. Or eye. Then I waited. And waited. There is a lot of waiting in show business, at least in my experience. A lot. So this wasn't unexpected.

What was unexpected was that the story I had invented and the subsequent feature-length screenplay I had wrought from it would end up triggering such a far-reaching explosion of uproar and chaos. By the time the brutal melee had ground itself to an ignominious end, it would be responsible for derailing ten long years of my life, which sent me spinning into a prolonged, rabid, frothing, self-destructive downward spiral. It would also end up incurring over *$5 million* in legal fees, turn my attorney into the California Lawyer of the Year, permanently change American copyright law and the way Hollywood itself does business on a daily basis, ignite a global Texas Hold'em explosion, be covered extensively by every major media news outlet on the planet, including, but not limited to, the *New York Times*, the *Los Angeles Times*, the Associated Press, CBS,

NBC, ABC, *Variety*, *The Hollywood Reporter*, and NPR, launch several major careers, and make not myself, but many others, very, very rich.

CHAPTER 2

THE DEAL

SO WHAT ARE WE TALKING about here, anyway? Why did this particular court case garner so much attention and ignite such a prolonged media firestorm? Surely, this type of thing must be fairly commonplace; we live in a highly litigious society. There's certainly no shortage of lawyers and lawsuits in modern-day America, so what made this *Grosso v. Miramax* case so newsworthy? Well, it was mainly due to an ingenious application of an intellectual property argument that my lawyer instituted called "breach of implied contract." Prior to my lawsuit, this particular approach didn't exist in these types of cases; *Grosso v. Miramax* was the first time it was used to any effect. And it worked. It worked like gangbusters. For a while.

Let me back up for a second. What happened was, when I originally sued Miramax for stealing my *Shell Game* script and turning it into *Rounders*, the case was tossed right out of court. It was summarily dismissed without so much as a nod or a whimper, which I will expound upon further in a later chapter. This was a tremendous blow at the time, as you can imagine, but in reality, it was just one of many crazy turns that this case took along its arduous and circuitous route. Nonetheless, we had lost, it seemed, right off the bat. "Sorry, Charlie, nice try. Go home," was the message. The case was immediately dismissed by the court as having no merit whatsoever. We were through, it seemed, just like that. However, as luck would have it, the battle didn't end there. Oh, no. Not even close. As it turned out, the fight was only just beginning...

Once the case was dismissed by the first judges who reviewed it (and it seemed to be all over, hopes dashed, etc.), lo and behold, my bright shark of a lawyer, John Marder, God bless him, worked himself up into some sort of three-piece-suit state of satori and conjured up a bona fide "breach of implied contract" legal epiphany, which led to us appealing that initial dismissal. That's right, we didn't fold like a wimpy house of cards, so to speak, in the face of one bad ruling. We were made of tougher stuff than that. We appealed the dismissal on these new "breach of implied contract" grounds that no one had ever heard of before, at least not in this type of case, and we won. All of the sudden, out of nowhere, Papa had a brand new bag. And this bag had teeth. We were successful in our appeal. The appellate court decided that in my particular case there was an "extra element" present. This "extra element," the "breach of implied contract" angle, gave us new life.

Now, one thing you have to understand is that prior to my case it was very difficult for writers in Hollywood, and elsewhere, to protect their ideas. As long as a studio, producer, network, or whomever, didn't shoot your script exactly as it was written, word for word, you had virtually no recourse if they decided to steal your characters, settings, events, themes, and what have you. Before *Grosso v. Miramax*, you couldn't really sue someone for stealing your ideas; the thieves just got away with it scot-free. Ideas, astonishingly enough, had no protection of any kind or very little. They could take pretty much whatever they wanted from a writer, no matter how long and hard that writer may have worked on the story or how near and dear it was to their heart and use it with no worries about repercussions of any kind. Seems crazy, I know, but that's how it was. The system was set up to favor the studios and those in power while keeping the struggling artist types right where they belonged: struggling.

My case changed all that. When my hot-shot lawyer dropped his "breach of implied contract" bomb, there was a seismic shift in the dirty Hollywood landscape and in the law. What this really meant was that any time a writer offered a studio, production company, network, or other such entity a creative work, there was an "implied contract" present, so that if they used that writer's idea or ideas, the writer should be compensated. With such an implied contract automatically in place, simply because the meeting or phone call or script submission had taken place, failure to compensate the writer—should the writer's material be used to produce a commercial product—would be a breach of that contract. Sounds fair enough, right? Sure, to you and me maybe, but in actuality, it was a highly controversial suggestion and one that ruffled a lot of feathers.

Well, the 9th Circuit Court of Appeals evidently agreed with Marder and allowed my case to go forward, overruling the original dismissal. This landmark ruling set a brand-new precedent and actually changed American copyright law. I kid you not. You can look it up. "Gloogle it," (sic) as my Uncle Tricky used to say. It also caused my name to be freshly inscribed in all the law books, scared the hell out of a lot of entertainment executives, and generated a ton of press, as I mentioned earlier.

Some of the articles that appeared lauded the decision as being a boon for writers, who now had more protection for their ideas, more recourse, and more "power" than ever before. Others took the exact opposite stance, saying that now it would be harder than ever for writers, screenwriters in particular, to get their projects in front of those with the ways and means to produce them. Which side was right? I honestly have no idea. "Both" seems to be the only answer, as both sides made valid points.

No matter which side you agree with, I think we can all agree that I can't really sit here and talk about how much news the damn case generated without providing some evidence to back it up. That would be unprofessional and irresponsible, and we here at *Dirty Dealing* are certainly neither of those....

On October 13, 2004, an article about the *Grosso v. Miramax, Rounders* court case appeared on the front page of *The New York Times* Arts section. No joke. The fucking *New York Times* Arts section. Front page. Heavy. Not only that, but the article just happened to be positioned in a vertical column that bordered a large photo of Bruce Springsteen (unrelated article), which I thought was pretty cool at the time, as I am a huge Boss fan. And although my article had no art (I'm not sure why, as I was more than ready for my close-up, but alas, sadly, no photographers ever showed up.), I still got a kick out of bordering the Boss in print.

"Look," I told anyone who'd listen, "I'm holding hands with Bruce in *The New York Times*." The article was written by Anne Thompson, with a headline that read, "Appeals Court Ruling May Shift Power to Writers," and it described how my lawsuit had just changed American copyright law. It also contained a very interesting quote, which went as follows: "'How bizarre that Disney and Miramax would allow this matter to become a case,' said Daniel H. Black of the Greenberg Traurig law firm. 'In situations like this, historically, it's not worth going to a judge. You settle quietly.'"[1]

How bizarre, indeed. Unless they knew that in the end, they really had no chance of losing, and they didn't want to set an example of paying off claims. But let's not get into all of that right here; it's a little early. We will dive deeper into this matter in a later chapter as well.

---

1   Anne Thompson, "Appeals Court Ruling May Shift Power To Writers," *New York Times*, October 13, 2004, https://www.nytimes.com/2004/10/13/movies/appeals-court-ruling-may-shift-power-to-writers.

The Associated Press picked up the story. This article appeared on both MSNBC.com and ABC.com and probably more places than those. It was titled "Million Dollar Ideas Often Stolen in Hollywood." It began as follows:

> "'Pirates of the Caribbean.' 'The Matrix.' 'The Last Samurai.' 'Broken Flowers.' 'Amistad.'"

> "Success isn't all that these films have in common. Each was also challenged by a lawsuit claiming 'idea theft'—a common Hollywood problem that lawyers say is likely to continue as long as huge movie studios wield enormous power.

> "'It's like having your soul ripped out,' says 37-year-old Cleveland resident Jeffrey Allan Grosso, who paid his way through film school by playing Texas Hold'em, wrote a screenplay about it, then sued Miramax over its poker movie 'Rounders.'

> "'All they would have had to do was give me a 'story by' credit,' Grosso says. 'They could have gotten me for nothing. I could have gone and used that credit to get other work. All I ever wanted to do was write movies.'

> "But why would movie studios, with every resource at their disposal, steal stories? Are

these writers just cranks, frustrated wannabes with delusions of creativity?

"No, says attorney John Marder, who specialized in representing aggrieved writers. Many are victims of a system that favors studios and networks and offers little protection for writers and ideas.

"'It's a small group of people that have all the juice, and if you're not in that crowd, you're really at their mercy,' he says. 'There's a real lack of moral compass on the issue in Hollywood. And there's an ego-driven arrogance about it, like how dare you challenge this producer, this director, this studio? They'll spend $10 million fighting a case where the demand is $100,000.'" (The Associated Press, via MSNBC.com, Nov. 9, 2006)

That was a pretty good one, even if some of the facts were wrong. I didn't go to film school, but I liked what that Grosso cat had to say—seems like he's really on the ball.... And I liked Marder's line about the "lack of moral compass." Saying there's a lack of moral compass in Hollywood is like saying there was a lack of lifeboats on the Titanic. Just ask ole Harvey Weinstein about that one.

The Wednesday, March 3, 2006 issue of *Daily Variety*, which is basically the Hollywood Bible, featured an article about the case on the cover of the magazine. The fucking cover, I kid you not. And this one even had a photo, although, typically and tragically, it was a pic of Matt Damon rather than the much more appealing and alluring *Shell Game* author. Shame. At any rate, it was written by Dave McNary and cleverly titled "Will Scribes Hold Cards?" It started as follows:

> *"An upcoming trial in Los Angeles may give Hollywood screenwriters the upper hand in disputes over whether their ideas have been stolen. The case stems from Miramax's 1998 film 'Rounders' and Jeff Grosso's suit alleging the mini-major ripped off his ideas about the world of underground poker from his 1995 script 'Shell Game.'*
>
> *"Key issue in the Grosso case, which goes to trial in July, is whether a contract is created when an executive hears a pitch or reads a screenplay—and there's the expectation that if the idea gets used, the writer will be paid.*
>
> *"Grosso's case could be a landmark because it differs significantly from typical screenwriter suits alleging copyright infringement. Usually, writers who are convinced their work has been stolen face a more difficult task in proving copyright infringement by establishing that the film was taken from*

the script's actual plot, dialogue, settings or characters.

"But Grosso achieved a key breakthrough in a 2004 federal court ruling. The 9th Circuit Court of Appeals turned down Miramax's motion to dismiss Grosso's claim that it violated its implied contract with Grosso— even though a federal court had dismissed the suit's copyright infringement allegations.

"'A contract sometimes may be implied even in the absence of an express promise to pay,' wrote Judge Mary M Schroeder in the ruling for the three-judge panel.

"Ruling meant that Grosso could proceed in state court with his lawsuit alleging Miramax breached his implied contract."[2]

Not bad, right? And yet even with all of the law changing and newsmaking, during the long course of the *Grosso v. Miramax* case, things didn't always go our way, to put it mildly. First of all, the case never went to trial. It never made it into an actual courtroom with jurors and whatnot. All of the judges' decisions were made "remotely," if you will. And there were some doozies, let me tell you. Not to

---

2   Dave McNary, "Will Scribes Hold Cards?"
     Variety, May 2, 2006, *https://variety.com/2006/biz/ markets-festivals/will-scribes-hold-cards-1200506453/.*

give away too much too soon, but just as a little teaser, on September 12, 2006, *The Hollywood Reporter* published an article that contained what was perhaps the most maddening single line in all of the judges' rulings on this case—one of the most maddening anyway, as there were several, as you will soon see.

The article was titled "Implied Contract Claims: No Agreement, No Breach" and contained a highly revealing and incomprehensibly frustrating line: "The court assumed, for purposes of the motion, that many of the same ideas were found in Grosso's script and Miramax's movie and that they may have had a 'common host.' Nevertheless, the court held that Grosso failed to raise a genuine issue of fact as to whether any agreement could be implied from the defendants' conduct."[3]

Hold the phone. What?! "A common host." The two works had "a common host." Isn't that rich? Well, seeing as I wrote my script in 1995, three years before *Rounders* was released, I certainly didn't steal it from them. Ergo, to-wit, therefore, I was the common host. Ole Sasqy, as I am sometimes known, host extraordinaire. What that statement meant was, that both works—my *Shell Game* screenplay and their *Rounders* movie—could have derived from one singular place, namely, me. Can you freaking believe that one? To this day, it makes me want to put my head through a wall.... But let's take a breath here before we get too excited. We'll wander into the phantasmagoric miasma

---

3   Aaron Moss, "Implied Contract Claims: No Agreement, No Breach," The Hollywood Reporter, September 12, 2006.

of all this a little bit further on down the trail. This is just an introduction to the story, after all, so let's not get carried away. I tend to get a tad hot when I revisit some of these old articles, as you can probably tell, and this is no time for me to lose my cool. We still have a lot more story to tell.

CHAPTER 3

THE BAIT

MY NAME IS JEFFREY ALLAN GROSSO. I was born July 1, 1969 in the small Northeastern hamlet of Willimantic, Connecticut. Willimantic was formerly an industrial town with a population of about 20,000. The original primary employer was the American Thread textile factory that closed in the 1970s. The reason we lived there, though, had nothing to do with yarn and everything to do with the fact that Willimantic was the nearest town to the University of Connecticut (UCONN), where my parents were both enrolled just prior to my birth. However, when it came time for me to go to college some seventeen years later, I did not follow in their footsteps. I chose a distinctly alternate path, one informed almost solely, surprising as it may sound, by the great game of poker.

I was first taught how to play poker by my paternal grandmother when I was five years old. The first hands I ever played were dealt across the cream and tan patterned

Formica table that sat like a monument in the kitchen of my grandparents' small, post-war suburban house in Fairfield, Connecticut. My grandparents were second generation Italian American; my grandfather was from Napoli and my grandmother from Sicily. On the wall of their bedroom hung one of those old, oval, black-and-white framed portraits of my grandmother's Sicilian parents, my great-grandparents. Both husband and wife were no more than five feet tall, and both were shaped like beer kegs. The stern, unsmiling expressions they bore harkened clearly to a serious life of duty and struggle.

When I was a child, my parents would often drop me off at my grandparents' Fairfield house for the weekend. It was during these weekends that I learned how to play card games of all kinds, poker being one of them.

My grandparents played cards regularly with my great aunts and uncles who lived nearby, particularly on the weekend evenings. There would be about eight of us seated around the kitchen table, and of course coffee and home-made cake was served. They all found it a little perplexing (but cute) that I always wanted to join in. In fact, a lot of the games I instigated myself through incessant begging and pleading. If it was up in the air whether or not there would be a game on a given night, I always made sure that the idea landed squarely in the kitchen. The next young-est person at the table was at least fifty years my senior, but I enjoyed these games tremendously. Poker, of course, was my favorite. We played for pennies. My grandmother had a tan, vinyl, draw-stringed cinch sack she had gotten in Las Vegas that had a large dollar sign printed on it, and it was in this sack that she kept her pennies. I worshipped that penny sack like it was the Lost Ark of the Covenant and the Holy Grail combined. All the aunts and uncles had similar receptacles that held their own pennies, which they would bring with them. No one ever spent their pennies, and no significant amounts of money were ever won or lost. It was just for fun, but technically we were gambling, if on a harmless level. Nevertheless, it was during these cake-and-coffee-filled congenial evenings of my youth that I learned how to play and bet and call and raise. And win. And lose.

I continued to play poker regularly all through my young adulthood. As a kid, I had yet to hear about the specific game of Texas Hold'em, but like a lot of kids I played in nickel-dime-quarter poker games with my friends all through junior high and high school. I loved it just as much as I did when I was sitting at my grandparents' kitchen table. I played every chance I could. We played 5- and 7-card Stud, Follow the Queen, 7-card Draw, and Baseball, games that usually included a plethora of wild cards.

Further feeding my hunger, I had an Uncle Tony, my father's brother, who happened to live in Las Vegas. Toward the end of my junior year of high school, I somehow convinced my mother to let me fly out there and visit him solo over spring break.

Vegas was a revelation. I took to the culture like a proverbial duck to water. And even though I was only seventeen years old, I was quite tall. This fact, coupled with the accidentally altruistic assistance of a thrillingly lackadaisical security philosophy, allowed me to gamble freely in the casinos without getting hassled.

The first day I was there, Uncle Tony took me for a tour of all the casinos on the strip. We were walking through the Dunes, which is now long since gone, along with most of the other original Strip casinos. They have all been systematically blown up and torn down to make way for bigger, better, more modern pleasure palaces. Random pangs of sentimentality aside, I don't find this progress to be necessarily a bad thing. To be perfectly honest, a lot of those old places were toilets. The new ones that replaced them are a lot nicer and have a lot more to offer. Do I occasionally miss the old days, when everything but gaming was virtually free and there was a much more prevalent human element to the town? Sure, occasionally. But not enough to want to trade the Wynn back in for the Desert Inn. Or the Bellagio for the Dunes, for that matter. I love the Bellagio. They have that insane lake and fountain outside and that big decorative flower sculpture room in the lobby that changes with the seasons, which is nothing short of amazing to witness at any time. What's not to like? But back in 1986, the Bellagio was still just a twinkle in Steve Wynn's eye, and my uncle and I were making our way through the casino floor of the still-erect Dunes. After meandering for a while through the seemingly endless maze of slot pits and table games, we turned a corner and happened upon a bank of ten-cent video poker machines that actually accepted dimes.

In direct contrast to how it is now, once upon a time, Las Vegas was a very coin-centric town. If you were a traditional Las Vegas devotee in those days, it was all about quarters, half dollars, silver dollars, and yes, even nickels and dimes. The sublime, bell-ringing sound that these physical coins made while bouncing off—in lightning-fast, staccato succession—the loud and echoing metal of the payout tray when you won any kind of jackpot was a big part of the allure. There may have only been a few dollars being spit out at any given time, but the obnoxiously loud and dramatic nature of the sonic assault made it sound like you were going to be rich for life. You felt like you had really accomplished something. Vegas has since been rendered almost entirely coin-free, and this glorious, ear-tingling, metal-on-metal clanging sensation, so ubiquitous for so long, has since been sadly replaced by a far less satisfying electronic substitution. The machines still make noise, it's just not the same kind of noise. It's soft, subdued, and musical. It's not visceral. It's not "real." And hence, nowhere near as wonderful.

Back in the day, handing the cashier a heavy bucket full of coins was a big part of the satisfaction of winning. The cashier would gruntingly lift and dump the bucket into the receptacle dish of the automatic coin counter, which looked a bit like a big coffee roaster, and the machine would vociferously tally your total. Then the cashier would pay you out. In cash. By hand. It was a tremendously gratifying high. Nowadays when you win, the machines spit out nothing more than a quiet and narrow slip of printed paper. Paper you then take and feed into an equally impersonal, unmanned kiosk that cashes you out through an unremarkable ATM-like slot in a humorless, expressionless, expedient fashion devoid of human charm of any kind. It's just not the same thing.

In 1986, however, coins were still very much in play in Vegas and at the Dunes. Conveniently, when I came across the bank of ten-cent video poker machines, I just happened to have two lonely dimes in my pocket. Having already been paraded by countless festively colored and beckoning inanimate one-armed bandits of all kinds for hours, I was finally unable to resist the siren call for a moment longer. I gave a quick glance around for security and, finding the coast clear, nonchalantly popped two dimes into the video poker machine directly in front of me. Once the dimes had been adequately swallowed, I excitedly pressed the "deal" button to start the game. The virtual cards, in all their colorful fantasticalness, came flying across the screen right on cue. I was dealt the ten of clubs, the king of clubs, and the ace of clubs, along with two other worthless cards that were of no help to me. Tony, oblivious to my unauthorized endeavor, continued to walk ahead of me through the casino and clear out of sight without even noticing that I had put any money into this machine. No matter. I would catch up with him in a minute. This first ever attempt at adult gaming was well worth the somewhat unsettling separation that was transpiring between me and the only person in my group who had any idea where we were or how to get out.

I, of course, inherently knew the basic rules of poker and the objective of the game, so I kept the three big clubs, disdainfully discarded the other two cards, and drew two new ones to take their place. And would you believe, as God as my witness, the two cards I drew were the jack and queen of clubs. This gave me a royal flush, the absolute best hand you can possibly achieve in poker. The ultimate goal of the game. Easy and pretty as you please. First time I had ever put a single cent in a machine of any kind. A royal flush. The best thing that can happen. The ultimate nuts. The jackpot.

Well, as soon as it hits, sirens start wailing, lights start flashing, and the other patrons are craning their necks to see what all the commotion is about. The change girls are alerted, and suddenly, somehow, out of nowhere, Uncle Tony is right back by my side. Without a word, he violently shoves me out of the way and takes my place in front of the machine. He knew that I was underage and had no ID proclaiming otherwise. He also knew that the casino would use that fact as a reason not to pay me. So, like a linebacker, he shoved me about ten feet across the carpet. I got the hint clearly and stayed away. A few minutes later, the floor-person came and congratulated him and with no fuss or muss, paid him the whopping sum of fifty dollars. In cash. From my twenty-cent investment. But as we breached the front doors into the freedom of the street and my uncle laughingly handed me the fifty, all I could think about—besides the fact that I had just magically transformed two dimes into a fifty-dollar bill like a goddamned wizard—was that if I had put in five dimes instead of two, the payout would have been $500.

Such is life. And make no mistake about it, that's how they get you. Furthermore, I will tell you this: I have played a lot of video poker since that day, and despite countless, innumerable hours of trying, I have never once hit another royal flush.

Crazy instances of beginner's luck aside, the real reason I was out there was not to mess around with dumb machines but to play some real, live-action poker against real, live-action players.

Hard to believe as it may sound now, at that time you couldn't find a live Texas Hold'em game in a Las Vegas casino with a poker-intentioned divining rod. There just weren't any. They didn't spread it anywhere. Absolutely nowhere. It didn't exist. Of course, Hold'em hasn't really been around that long. It's a relatively new version of poker. Texas Hold'em was only invented in the late 1950s, and the first year the World Series of Poker was held at the Horseshoe Casino in downtown Las Vegas—featuring No-Limit Hold'em as its main event—was 1970. It was a new game for a new time.

Now, of course, it's ubiquitous. These days it's just about the *only* game you can find, no matter where you go. It has quickly and efficiently supplanted all the other games like a dominating virus. Not to mention the fact that you can't channel surf the nether reaches of the cable dial at any time, day or night, without seeing it played live on TV. It's on multiple channels at all hours. Plus, the internet. There are tournaments of all kinds being shown from all over the world constantly. 24/7/365. It's unbelievable. It's absolutely everywhere, all the time. That's how fast the game grew. Ridiculously fast. Exponentially fast. But why?

Two factors are generally considered to be the reasons behind the Hold'em boom. One was Chris Moneymaker (great name) winning the 2003 World Series of Poker. He qualified for the tournament by winning an online "satellite" tournament that had cost him eighty-six dollars to enter. A satellite tournament is a generally low-dollar tournament you play in to try to win entrance into a more prestigious, high-dollar tournament. Instead of winning cash, you win a seat in a bigger event, which you likely could otherwise not afford to enter. From his eighty-six dollar buy-in for the online satellite tournament, upon taking first place out of thousands of players, Moneymaker won the $10,000 buy-in for the World Series of Poker tournament in Vegas. The main event. The biggest poker tournament in the world. That WSOP tournament he won his entry fee into, was, remarkably, the first time he had ever played in a live poker tournament in person with real people. He went on to win it, somehow, and take home the $2.5 million cash prize, plus a very nice gold bracelet. The victory made him instantly famous and fanned the flames of a Hold'em wildfire that had been sparked five years earlier in 1998 with the release of the poker movie *Rounders*. In fact, Moneymaker tells anyone who will listen that *Rounders* was the reason he started playing No-limit Hold'em in the first place. And since *The Shell Game* was the source of *Rounders*, well, you can do the math.

Back in 1986, however, on my spring break trip to Vegas in my junior year of high school, there was no Hold'em to be found. It had yet to take root and spread. I ended up playing one-to-four dollar 7-card Stud at the famed Stardust Casino every day and most of the nights during that visit. 7-card Stud was the game everyone played then. If there were three tables going in the Stardust poker room at that time, they were all 7-Stud games. So I played 7-Stud. I played a lot of it. And I ended up winning. Not much of course, but I wound up leaving Vegas with a couple hundred dollars more than I had when I arrived. And a couple hundo wasn't bad for an awkward, seventeen-year-old greenhorn in 1986. It was my first real, live poker experience in a proper card room, at a proper felt-covered, nine-seat table with proper metal-centered poker chips, and a proper surly, disaffected dealer. Needless to say, I was hooked. This being the case, hook planted firmly in my fish mouth, when it came time for me to choose a college, I had other things besides just receiving a good education informing my selection process.

Although UCONN was the de facto, state-sponsored, easy choice for the large majority of college-bound seniors at my Willimantic, CT high school, I made the rather unlikely and somewhat unpopular decision not to attend the local U. Whilst I did dutifully apply there and was accepted into the honors program, I never really had any intention of attending UCONN.

Unbeknownst to those around me, I was steely-eyed in my determination to venture as far away as I could from the endless grass, trees, and boredom of Connecticut, and I had made motions toward that end. I had applied and was accepted to other schools, including, fortunately for me, Pepperdine University in Malibu, CA. Pepperdine appealed to me on several levels. First, it was located as far away as was geographically possible from Connecticut while still remaining inside the mainland United States. Second, I had always dreamt of California as both a state and a state of mind, and I was anxious to explore the lifestyle I had read about in books and seen on TV and film. Third, Pepperdine just happened to sit on a hillside overlooking Malibu Beach. And last, but certainly not least, I had read in a book that poker was actually legal in certain counties in Southern California. I remember being astounded when I read this. There was no blackjack or roulette. There were no slot machines or video poker. There were no craps tables. But regular table poker had somehow skirted the law as a "game of skill" rather than a "game of chance" and was at some point miraculously rendered legal in certain specific magical places in Los Angeles County. A mysterious and floral-sounding town called Gardena kept popping up as the locale of some of these "card clubs." Gardena seemed to be the main hub of this unlikely legal poker action.

Hence, a year after that spring break trip, when I was a high school senior and faced with the prospect of going away to college, I suppose I don't need to tell you what was on my mind. The gears, as they say, were turning. The idea that I could be legitimately pursuing my degree in creative writing and at the same time playing live-action money poker just a short drive away sounded just about like heaven to me. And I could be doing all this while living in Malibu Beach, of all places. And so I went, knowing nothing and no one, having never even visited the campus. I landed at LAX by myself, just barely eighteen and green as a tree frog, alone, having never been to LA before, and ecstatically free for the first time in my life. It took me no time at all to buy a car—a white, 1969 Mustang coupe I purchased for $2,600 derived from selling my baseball card collection—and not much more than a moment after that to find the poker clubs in Gardena. I was drawn there like I was enveloped in a tractor beam.

I played poker to support myself through college, but it was really more of an obsession than a moneymaking pastime, hobby, or "job." I played pretty much every waking moment I could and sometimes even while I was asleep. Right from my freshman year, 1987–88, I was at the Normandie Card Club in Gardena far more than I was at school. And it stayed that way until I graduated. I started out playing 7-card Stud as I had during that spring break in Vegas, but I started noticing very quickly that the tables on the other side of the card room were populated with a wilder variety of player. They were constantly screaming and yelling and fighting with each other, accusations and insults of all kinds perpetually flying in a torrent of indistinguishable languages.

Occasionally, things got so heated that objects would be hurled. It wasn't unusual to glance up toward the nicotine-stained ceiling tiles late on a Friday night and see chicken bones and other handy projectiles sailing through the rising smoke like airplanes taking off and landing on a foggy evening at nearby LAX. You could still smoke in the clubs in those days, and everybody did. They smoked like fiends. Often, they would have two chokes going at a time, one in each ashtray on either side of them. I would say something like, "Uh, would you mind putting just one of those out? The smoke is drifting up right into my face."

"So? Change tables," was the usual reply.

The atmosphere, particularly on that side of the room, smacked more of an Old West saloon than a modern, civilized card room or casino. Fistfights broke out regularly. The security guards stayed busy. But most importantly for me, huge pots were forming regularly in the center of these tables. Giant, Krakatoa-sized mountains of chips were rising from the fertile green felt, seemingly almost every hand. Mountains of money that were totally up for grabs. Mountains so big I could spot their peaks from clear across the room. Small farm animals were being lost in these pots. Not literally, of course, but you get the idea. The 7-Stud pots rarely grew to even half that size. You could barely hide a cockroach from the kitchen in our pots. So, naturally, I became curious.

"What game is that?" I innocently asked my dealer. "Over there, where everybody is jumping around and yelling."

"Texas Hold'em," he replied. "You don't want no part of that."

"No? Why not?" I queried.

"Too fast. Too much action. You can go broke real quick," he said.

"You don't say…."

At that moment, I pretty much jumped up from my Stud seat, tossed the dealer a buck for luck, and ambled over to an empty seat at a three-to-six-dollar-limit Hold'em table. And that, my friend, was the flashpoint. And the fire was lit.

CHAPTER 4

THE FISH

EVEN NOW, SOME THIRTY YEARS down the twisted, obstacle-strewn road, I can still recall the very first hand of Texas Hold'em I was ever dealt. I can remember it like I can remember the first time I rode a bicycle without training wheels. My father pushed me along, running beside me while holding onto the back of the seat. Once I was really moving, he let go. I flew straight and solo for a few wondrous seconds, riding high and mighty into the mysterious, beckoning fantasy of freedom, then inexplicably turned left down a sloping driveway and crashed into a dumpster. But I survived and recovered to ride again.

The only other time in my life I've ever been blessed with that free and floating feeling of soaring victory was at the poker table. I'm not going to go on record and say anything goofy like "It's better than sex," but I will say that raking in a huge pile of chips after winning a big hand or taking first place in a tournament is better than any high

I've ever received from any drug I've ever taken (not that I've tried them all). Winning a huge pot or being the last man standing in a tournament is definitely its own kind of drug. It absolutely gets you high and is extremely addictive. When you rake in and stack in front of you the chips won in a big pot—chips that just seconds earlier belonged to your opponents—or are presented with a bundle of cash and a trophy following a tournament victory, you can't help but get as high as the ever-present moon. For that brief moment in time, you are solely victorious. You feel invincible, like anything is possible and the entire world is nothing more than a dumb, round rock just waiting for you to conquer it. Of course, this feeling, beautiful as it may be, like everything else in life, is fleeting. Soon it will wear off and you will need another fix.

The great thing about poker is the purely democratic nature of it. The cards don't care if you're white, black, brown, orange, gay, straight, questioning, old, young, tall, short, thin, fat, male, female, or anything in between. Everyone with a hand in front of them starts out on an equal and level playing field. Everyone faces the same odds, and the only elements in between you and winning are luck and skill. You don't have to wait two weeks for a paycheck. You don't have to clock-watch the slow, excruciating minutes tick by to accrue your measly hourly wage. You don't have to rely on a rigged stock market to go up or down. The money is sitting right there in the middle of the table. Every hand. Over and over again. All you have to do is reach out and take it.

The poker table is a totally egalitarian society. A captain of industry might be sitting next to a housewife, who might be sitting next to a gang member, who might be sitting next to a shady lawyer, who might be sitting next to a ninety-year-old retired railroad engineer, who might be sitting next to a seventeen-year-old student with a good fake ID. It's a melting pot in the truest sense, and no one is judged by anything more or less than the size of their chip stack and the cards in their hand. No one cares about anything except who won and who lost, and once that has been decided, moving on to the next hand. There is no discrimination, no bigotry, no racism, no sexism, no ageism...no isms of any kind. Even if the players are all racist, sexist, egotistical bigots at home or on the street, at the poker table, all that matters are cards and money. The rest is left at the door.

The very first hand of Texas Hold'em poker I ever played was dealt to me over a three-to-six-dollar limit table at the famed Normandie Card Club in Gardena, California. I was dealt ten-six offsuit, meaning the two cards in my hand were two different suits. I held the ten of clubs and the six of diamonds. It was my turn to act, and I had no idea what to do. I had bought in and sat down at the table, somewhat unwisely, without even knowing how the game was played. I was so anxious to be a part of it, I hadn't even taken the time to learn the rules.

In poker terminology, a "fish" is the sucker at the table, the player that all the sharps and sharks anxiously sniff out, attack, destroy, cut up, and eat. At that moment, I was the ultimate fish. I sat there, staring at my two cards, which held very little meaning for me, nervously wondering what I should do. To compound matters further, I was totally unused to the pace of the game, which was much faster than the 7-Card Stud version of poker I was used to playing at that time.

Perhaps I should mention that I had only just turned eighteen years old, even though the legal gambling age was, and is, twenty-one. I was also a freshman in college in a land where I knew no one, a strange and foreign land that sprawled out in an infinite expanse of stucco, cement, and hard white light, a land populated with a densely packed variety of humanity to whom I'd had no prior exposure. I was decidedly out of my element, but not as much as you might think. Even at eighteen, I'd already had limited experience playing live action poker in a casino setting, and I'd played a ton of it in home games all throughout my youth. But I had never played this particular game of Texas Hold'em before. Admittedly, it wasn't the coolest idea to jump into the shark-infested waters without even knowing how to swim.

In the Texas Hold'em incarnation of poker, each player is dealt just two cards at the outset. These two cards are dealt face down to each player and are called "hole cards." Once the players receive these two initial cards, they then must decide whether they wish to play the hand by putting chips in the pot or fold and toss their cards back to the dealer. This decision is normally made by the quality of the two cards in your hand. Big cards are generally better than small cards. Suited cards, say the queen and king of hearts, are better than unsuited cards, like my ten-six, and pairs, especially big pairs, are considered premium starting hands. "Premium" meaning that your odds of winning are increased in tandem with the quality of your starting hand. The better your first two cards are, the better the odds that you will end up with the best hand once all the cards are dealt out.

This is not entirely unlike life itself. The better the hand you are dealt at birth, the better your chances are of succeeding in life, generally speaking. The privileged tend to stay privileged and the underprivileged tend to stay underprivileged, which is unfortunate. However, the silver lining is that this is not always the case. In Hold'em, as in life, the best starting hand does not always win. Not hardly. The absolute best starting hand you can receive, perhaps obviously, is two aces, which is sometimes referred to in poker lingo as "pocket rockets." But holding a pair of aces as your first two cards in no way ensures you will win the hand. At a nine-seat poker table, a player who starts with a pair of aces will end up with the best hand less than half the time. This leaves a lot of wiggle room for other cards to sneak in and steal your lunch, which they will invariably do.

You can, of course, win a hand, or many hands, of Hold'em with even the crummiest of cards. This is commonplace. You can get lucky, or you can bluff. This is all part of the game. But still, the good players, the smart players, generally try to start off with two good cards, thus increasing their chances of raking in the chips in the end. As mentioned above, these first two cards are known as hole cards, and are dealt to each player face down, so no player knows the other players' hole cards. These two initial cards remain a mystery until they are revealed at end of the hand in the "showdown," assuming the hand progresses that far.

After the first two hole cards are dealt, and the first round of betting action has been completed, the dealer then puts out three cards in the middle of the table. These are dealt face up for everyone to see and are community cards that are shared by all the players. For instance, if a player has two hearts in their hand and the dealer puts out three hearts on the "board"—the name for the community cards spread in the middle—that player would have a flush. If another player in the same hand held two kings and one of the hearts on the board was the king of hearts, that player would have three kings.

These first three cards the dealer spreads out face up are known as "the flop." Then there is another round of betting, after which the dealer puts out a single card next to the original three. This fourth card is called the "turn" card. The players now have four community cards they can work with, in addition to their own individual starting two, in order to make their best five-card hand. A poker hand consists of five cards. No more and no less.

After the turn card is dispensed and another round of betting ensues, the dealer puts out one last card. This is called the "river" card. After this fifth and final card is placed on the board, there is one last round of betting, after which the winner is declared—again, assuming the hand progresses that far.

A player's final hand is determined by the best five-card hand they can make out of the seven available cards. Sometimes only one hole card is utilized, sometimes both, and sometimes none. In the latter case, it means the player is simply "playing the board." This whole process unfolds rapidly. Texas Hold'em is a fast-moving game, which lends to its appeal. When playing 7-Card Stud, for instance, you can pretty much eat an entire plate of fried calamari and read a chapter of *Fear and Loathing in Las Vegas* in the time the players take to make a move. No one is in any kind of rush. But Hold'em is different. If 7-Card Stud is a lumbering cruise ship, Hold'em is a wave-skipping speed boat.

Almost immediately upon receiving my ten-six offsuit starting hand that night at the Normandie Club, I was under extreme pressure from the dealer and the other players to decide whether I was going to call, raise, or fold. I was already unnerved just sitting there, and this browbeating from the dealer only made matters worse. I was frozen. Cold beads of sweat formed on my forehead. I was shaky and twitchy. I had no idea what move I should make, all the while internally condemning myself for not having learned how to play the game before I sat down. I was impulsive by nature, I suppose.

At that moment, with my mind confused and racing, I was reminded of a conversation I once had with one of my oldest and dearest friends who bears the odd moniker of Logan Cutlip. "Jeff," he said, in response to some crazy story or another I had just related to him, "you live your life like a hot rod screaming down the freeway at a hundred and fifty miles an hour with no rearview mirror and no brakes."

This assessment never seemed more accurate than at this particular moment. At the ever-increasing insistence of the dealer, I was forced to make a decision. Without really even thinking about it, I folded my hand, tossing my cards into the "muck pile," which is the name for the accumulation of the sad and discarded hands of the players who have folded. Both my cards and my head were in the muck pile. But I figured it was better to err on the side of caution. I had no idea whether I had done the right thing or not, but I was relieved just to be out of the hot seat. My peace would not last long.

As if on cue, the three shared community cards of the flop came ten, ten, six. Had I kept my hand and called the initial bet, rather than nervously folding, this flop would have given me an instant full house—which is three of one card and two of another, e.g. three tens and two sixes. More than that, I would have held what they call the "nut" hand, meaning that it was the best hand one could possibly achieve with that particular spread of cards on the board.

I would have had the nuts. Instead, I went nuts. For I then had to sit there and watch in helpless agony as the rest of the hand played out and the pot grew and grew and grew. Bet. Raise. Re-raise. And all of this happening with six or seven players still in the hand. Hence, there were lots and lots of chips being tossed into the ever-mounting pot. By the end, the mound of chips in the center of the table had grown to over $200, and the winning hand ended up being a pocket pair of eights. I would have won easily. Even though it turns out I had unwittingly actually made the "right" or "proper" move by folding, as ten-six offsuit is a pretty lousy hand, I was aghast. If I wasn't hooked already, I sure as heck was then.

I loved playing Hold'em, and after I navigated a few sharp turns of the learning curve, I got pretty good at it pretty quickly. Soon, I was raking in large pots of my own on a regular basis. I became totally enthralled with the game, and it wasn't long before I was at the Normandie Club more than I was on campus.

After a little trial and error, I had trained myself into becoming a winning Hold'em player. It really wasn't that hard back then because the opponents I faced at any given table were generally not very good poker players. In fact, most of them were downright awful. Thank God. So I was able to win. Not always and not a lot, but frequently and enough. To put it in context, I was making a hell of a lot more scratch than I would have been able to earn flipping burgers or waiting tables or what have you. As a result, even as a "starving" freshman college student, I pretty much always had a wad of disposable cash on me. I was big pimping, so to speak, in my own subdued fashion. But it was a distinctly antisocial enterprise for me in those days. The other kids on campus and my dormmates in particular, to whom I was closest, were all busy doing normal college stuff. Meanwhile, I was gone most of the time, hanging out at a place they didn't know existed, doing something that they couldn't even comprehend. And I was keeping very odd hours.

As a freshman at Pepperdine, having just turned eighteen, I would drive to the Normandie Card Club on a typical Friday night in my white V-8 1969 Mustang coupe. I would arrive at the club alone, glaringly underage, and play Hold'em all night in the smoke until the sun came up. Given today's modern cultural environment, where you can get hung by your thumbs in the public square for even thinking about lighting up *outside* in Los Angeles, it's hard to even accurately convey the sheer industrial density of the cigarette smoke that filled the poker clubs in those days. At times, it was so bad your eyes would burn, and you could barely read your cards through the haze. It was as if the smoke and the oxygen had fought a war, the oxygen lost, and was subsequently banished, permanently exiled to the bubbles of carbonation in the soft drinks.

Perhaps that's why I never got carded. Being so tall, the security guards couldn't see my face, as it resided in the higher altitudes where the ascending smoke made it impossible to recognize facial features. My head was obscured by toxic clouds, and these were very stinky clouds. By the time I got back to campus, my clothes always reeked to high heaven. You could smell me coming down the hall. I was like a six-foot-five walking ashtray.

The Normandie club itself was located where the Harbor Freeway meets Rosecrans Boulevard in the city of Gardena, California. In those days, it took exactly the length of Bruce Springsteen's *Born to Run*—thirty-seven minutes—to get there from Pepperdine, as long as you didn't get caught in traffic. Despite its floral nomenclature, Gardena did not remind me of any garden I had ever seen. Not even remotely. If the devil himself decided he needed to take up a hobby to relax and started his own private garden in Hell, it would probably look a lot like Gardena. It was a sketchy section of town, to put it nicely. To put it not so nicely, it was a war zone. As such, the approach to and departure from the club was always an anxious run. I was a young kid from out of state driving an old car that was not as mechanically sound as would have been ideal, and I usually had a decent-sized roll on me. Yet despite a few frayed nerves, nothing ever really happened to me, and once you were in the club, you were pretty safe. The security guards were on top of things for the most part, and throughout my time there, I never encountered any real trouble, except from the cigarette smoke, flying chicken bones, and the occasional outraged opponent. Not to mention the perpetually looming cloud of catching cold cards, which I did encounter on more than one occasion. That was trouble enough. Not everyone, however, shared my relatively good fortune, as we will discover shortly.

Whether I had lost my bankroll or won a bundle, I would generally end up staggering across the elegantly landscaped Pepperdine campus toward my dorm from the upper parking lot in a total daze at 5 or 6 a.m., at which point I would crash and pretty much sleep all day.

While the other kids were all heading to the beach or taking joyrides up Sunset over to Westwood or just doing whatever it was that normal college kids did, I was dead to the world, recharging for my next session. Maybe here and there I was involved in some assorted activities, but for the most part, I was on a reverse schedule and spending the vast majority of my time that I wasn't in class at the Normandie Club. I was enjoying the action and fast money of the card room but simultaneously feeling socially and emotionally isolated from my classmates. In a word, I was lonely. As a result, I made an executive decision—one that still haunts me to this day. I agreed to teach my friend and dormmate, Munchy, how to play Hold'em. I just wanted someone to go to the club with; I just wanted some freaking company. I figured it would be a lot more fun if I had a partner rather than humping over there by myself all the time. Plus, it was a fairly sketchy trip, and having a shotgun rider sure wouldn't hurt, even a diminutive, goofball one. I'd had just about as much of the lone wolf lifestyle as I could take, and it wasn't like I was forcing anything on him. Munchy was more than willing to get involved. He was one of the few individuals on campus who knew what I was up to. He'd heard the stories, and he saw the cash firsthand. And so it was, one afternoon, as we sat on a single bed face to face in a Pepperdine dorm room, I taught Munchy how to play Texas Hold'em. (For the fictionalized version of this event as it appears in *The Shell Game* screenplay, see "Extra Bullet Three.")

It took all of about five seconds for Munchy to become totally hooked. It seemed like he fell into it even faster and harder than I did. But in his case, this was a bit of a problem, because it turned out that Munchy wasn't a very good poker player. In fact, he was terrible. I admittedly didn't have much patience back then as a young and wild whippersnapper, and I still don't. I'm perpetually wound-up by nature. But Munchy was far worse. Munchy had none.

For those of you unfamiliar with the game, in order to become a successful Texas Hold'em player on any level, you have to fold a lot of hands. By "fold a lot of hands," I mean that you have to fold immediately upon receiving your first two cards. If the initial hand you are dealt is sub-par, you have to dump it, toss it right in the muck pile before you put a single chip in the pot. Then you have to sit there like a lump and watch as the rest of the players at the table play out the hand, as I had done with my initial ten-six. This is the nature of the beast. Sure, it's still the greatest game in the world and at times can be more thrilling and exciting than just about anything you've ever done in your life, but there is also a fair amount of patience involved in being a winning poker player.

It's simple mathematics. In order to become a winning player and remain one in the long run, you should roughly be playing only 15 to 20 percent of the hands you are dealt. This number is debatable and may fluctuate somewhat depending on the other players at your table and the tone and temper of the game, but as a general rule of thumb, it is more or less an accurate figure for a nine-seat Limit Hold'em game. This means that you have to fold your hand before any action occurs, before the "flop," around 80 to 85 percent of the time. And while this prudent practice may result in the game not expressing itself as wall-to-wall meat-ball action every single minute you are sitting at the table—this can be challenging for even the best of us—it still seems simple enough, right? Just exercise a little patience, be a little smart, and win rather than play every hand and lose.

Well sure, it should be just that easy. And it can be. But when you're an eighteen-year-old drunken punk bouncing off the walls and suffer from chronic ADD, or ADHD, or ADDHHDDHD, or just general ants in your pants as Munchy did, it can go from challenging to impossible pretty quick. As I said, I wasn't exactly an expert at practicing any brand of patience myself. I for sure played more hands than I should have from time to time, if not always, but Munchy was on a whole other level. It was like he'd never even heard of the word "fold." Munchy played every hand, all the way, all the time. If there was even the slightest chance that he could pull off a miracle card that would give him even a minute chance of winning, no matter how long the odds, he played them all right to the end. "All the way to the river," as they say in the game.

What this meant in a real-world sense was that Munchy lost more than he won. Not that he didn't win occasionally; he did, but it was clear early on that while I was more or less a winning player, Munchy was a problem. As such, Munchy was constantly in debt to me, as I would have to loan him the money to put him in the games. While he did occasionally redeem himself temporarily by hitting something called a "bad beat jackpot," which was a random cash bonus the casinos handed out as a promotional marketing tool, these instances were few and far between.

In the bigger picture, Munchy was like a junkie whose drug of choice was the action of the Hold'em table. He was a junkie who always needed another fix and didn't often have the cash to pay for it. I only mention it because this fevered condition would end up drastically changing the course of his life and eventually cause him to land squarely in some pretty serious trouble. Trouble that would lead to him running around Los Angeles wearing a bulletproof vest and carrying a .38 caliber handgun with him whenever he left whatever "no-tell" motel he was currently calling home. Further, this was trouble that one could argue was all my fault, since I was the one who taught him how to play.

CHAPTER 5

THE DIVE

THROUGHOUT MY COLLEGE YEARS, HOLD'EM pretty much ruled my life. I was a stone-cold junkie for the action, no question about it. I played virtually every waking moment I could. I went to classes on occasion, but only the classes where attendance was mandatory and recorded, and for most of them, it wasn't. Most of them only required you to do the assignments and pass the tests. Some of them only required that you pass the final exam. Nothing else. You never even needed to show up at all. Can you imagine?

Not infrequently, I would walk into a final exam and the professor would ask me for my ID, not having the faintest clue as to who I was, as they hadn't seen me there a single time since the class began and they figured I was probably hired by some wealthy slacker student, of which there were many at Pepperdine, as a "ringer" to take their test for them. They would look at me sideways and suspicious, like, "Who the fuck are you?" I would then have to explain, a little bit ashamedly, granted, that I was legitimately enrolled in the class. It was fairly amusing. I got a kick out of it, anyway. And I never once failed a class. Although I did receive one D, in calculus, but that was simply due to a mental facility for higher math that had reached its limits. At any rate, as a result of all of this, I had a lot of free time on my hands to play poker at the clubs.

"But when did you study?" you may be wondering. Well, not very often and not very much, to be honest. Just enough to get by, really, which didn't amount to a whole lot. For instance, I never even bought textbooks. Well, that's not entirely true. Let me rephrase. I did spend $500 of my own hard-earned money buying books the very first semester of my freshman year. My parents' support, God bless them, combined with a partial scholarship and the obligatory student loans, while it lovingly and gratefully covered tuition and room and board, ended there. It didn't extend as far as the ridiculously overpriced textbooks we were "required" to purchase, nor anything else, hence the poker.

Feeling cheated almost immediately, I returned all the books a week later for a full refund, realizing I didn't need them. I was from New York, after all, or close enough. I knew a con when I saw one. I never bought books again, not a single one. Not ever. Even when I was winning at poker, I never spent another cent on a goddamned, worthless, hundred-dollar textbook. And I still managed to pass my classes.

"How?" Well, gumption, ingenuity, creativity, and wit. It wasn't even that hard. I was a decent writer, even back then, and that went a long way. With a little bit of focus and some well-placed minimal effort, you could pretty much bluff your way through anything. Nobody cared all that much. College, in my opinion, is overrated as a means of receiving a true education. That said, I wouldn't trade my experience there for anything in the world, and I learned a ton during my residence, only the majority of it wasn't gleaned from the professors hired to teach me. Not that I'm bad-mouthing the professors; I'm sure they all did their best. And proud we are of all of them.

Poker, much to the dismay of my guidance counselor and my put-upon girlfriend, Tiffany, was my main focus during those years and the source of not only my income, but most of my joy. Not that Tiffany wasn't a lovely girl, and I didn't enjoy her company. I very much did. My point is that not even the love of a gorgeous coed could distract me or dissuade me from the poker table.

Now, you might find this hard to believe, but the summer following my sophomore year at Pepperdine, both of my parents told me not to come home. When I called to inform them that the semester was ending and I was ready to book my plane ticket back to the eastern woods, they both said that they were busy, and I was not welcome. Each one, independently. It was unbelievable. My mother said, "Well, you can't come here, call your father." And my father said, "Well, you can't come here, call your mother." It gave me a moment of pause, I must admit. I remember hanging up the phone and muttering something glib like, "Well, isn't that a fine how do you do?"

When the summer semester break comes, as any of you who have attended any college of any kind know all too well, you no longer have housing. You have nowhere to live. You are effectively evicted, as in, "Pack up your shit and go." Therefore, my ever-loving parents were basically telling me to hit the bricks, go away, and disappear into the wilderness of the wicked city. To this day, I'm not sure what their deal was. I was getting decent grades. I was passing all my classes. I hadn't done anything wrong, at least that they knew about, yet they wanted nothing to do with me. Go figure.

Whatever the reason, it put me in a tight spot. But rather than cry and complain and push the issue, I figured I'd better just make other plans and right quick. I was in a bit of a pickle, as I was looking at four months off and nowhere to go. After expressing my predicament to a few people, I was eventually informed that there was a program already in place for wayward souls such as myself. If you signed up, the school would allow you to stay on campus for free all summer and put you to work on one of the maintenance crews. That sounded okay to me, and even though Munchy was born and raised in the nearby San Gabriel Valley, his home life wasn't all that stellar either, so he agreed to join me. We were given one bedroom in a two-bedroom apartment, which we shared, and full-time jobs that paid four dollars an hour. The jobs consisted of changing light bulbs, repairing screens, painting, and other such menial maintenance chores. Most importantly, however, these mindless gigs kept us close to Normandie and right in the Hold'em groove. We were more into it than ever at that time, as we weren't even taking classes and these "jobs" required us to pretty much just show up in any condition we liked. There wasn't a ton of responsibility or oversight, to put it mildly.

As soon as Munchy and I started working on the maintenance crew, we adopted a rather extreme habit of heading to Normandie on Friday after work and playing Hold'em straight through until the last minute on Monday morning. We played around the clock for the entire weekend. No sleep. No showers. No breaks. We never left the club. And if we hit rush hour traffic returning to campus on Monday morning, as we invariably did, nodding off at the wheel on the 405, we were usually late for work. Luckily, no one seemed to care.

Munchy drove an old red convertible Volkswagen Beetle. It wasn't exactly in mint condition, nor was it particularly well maintained. (Here's a little fun fact you may not know: the VW Beetle, or Bug, favored mode of transport for the ultra-liberal Hippie generation, was conceived and designed by none other than Adolf Hitler, the mass murdering Fascist ruler of the Nazis. True story. You can look it up. Volkswagen, in German, translates to "car of the people.")

Lucky for us, one of the reasons that Bugs were so favored by Hippies and their ilk was that they were very simple and easy to repair. Munchy and I took turns driving to the club, and whenever it was his turn, it was always a coin flip as to whether we would make it there without incident. The Bug broke down in traffic on the freeway or in the middle of PCH plenty of times, and we would have to sit there like a rock while Munchy performed a quick MacGyver repair job. Other drivers would be leaning on their horns, whizzing around us, screaming profanities, and Munchy would be hopping around like a rabbit trying to fix the problem. It was more than a little unnerving, but he always insisted on driving half the time, and he was pretty good at fixing that car.

What he invariably did was run a long wire from the battery under the hood in the front, through the inside of the car, between the seats, out the back window, and down into the engine compartment, where he would affix it to the engine. I'm not exactly sure how the mechanics of it all worked, but he always managed to get us rolling again. After a five- or ten-minute fright-filled stall-out, we would continue on our way to our lovely weekend resort destination or back to campus for work, depending on which way we were headed. I mention all this only to express, in no uncertain terms, the almost unfathomable depth of our depravity. Please let this ludicrous routine that no sane person would ever dare attempt, let alone adopt for any length of time, serve to demonstrate just how dedicated we were to the game.

The best marathon poker session story I know involves Munchy when he decided, out of the blue and for no particular reason, that he was going to stay and play until he hit a bad beat jackpot, the random payout that the card clubs offered to entice players to stay and play at their club rather than at a rival club. This involved a very low-percentage outcome whereby a player would lose a very good hand (such as aces-full or four of a kind) to an even better hand (such as a larger four of a kind or a straight flush). When this miracle occurred, the lucky losing player in question was given a lump sum of cash generally consisting of several thousand dollars. The winning player also got a cut, usually around 30 percent of the total, and the rest of the players at the table all received a small piece as well, but the lion's share went to the player who "lost" the big hand.

Despite the extremely long odds, these jackpots were paid out fairly regularly, maybe once a week or so. This was mainly due to the fact that there were so many games going around the clock, day and night, each dealing around thirty hands an hour. Much like the lotto on a localized scale, someone was bound to hit one eventually. It just wasn't likely to be you.

Munchy had eyes for these jackpots like a hungry dog has eyes for a freshly cooked ham or a thirsty alcoholic has eyes for a bottle of gin. He was obsessed. So one day he announces that come hell or high water, he's going to play straight through until he hits one. No matter how long it takes. No matter how broke he goes. No matter how much he has to borrow. He's going to keep playing until he hits a bad beat jackpot.

I don't need to explain to you the absurdity of this notion. It far surpassed unrealistic and easily entered the realm of virtual impossibility. It entered right through the front door without even knocking. He could play for six months and never hit one. Years, even. Some regular players go their entire lives without ever hitting one. But no one was going to put him off his plan. He was determined, and as you can probably tell, he wasn't much for listening to reason. But that's what made Munchy, Munchy. That and the fact that he always seemed to be snacking on something while somehow maintaining a constant weight of 130 pounds. I always suspected that he adopted this perpetual snacking habit as a way of emulating his favorite fictional character, Rusty, played by Brad Pitt in the Soderbergh remake of *Ocean's Eleven*. Or maybe he was just hungry. It's hard to know, but it sure made a mess. You should have seen his dorm room. It was like a sitcom stage.

His roommate was a strait-laced Church of Christ disciple, immaculate as a neat freak can be, and Munchy was the ultimate slob of all time. They were like *The Odd Couple* junior. The room was divided in half, with the edge of Munchy's sprawling pile of dirty laundry and burrito wrappers on the floor serving as the amorphous demarcation line. Whenever it was time for us to go somewhere, Munchy would sniff through the knee-deep layer of refuse that covered the floor like a hound dog on a bone hunt, searching for his cleanest dirty shirt. Every inch of his side of the room was covered in dirty laundry, discarded books and papers, ravaged junk food wrappers, and soda cans. You couldn't even really walk around, while at the same time, the other half of the room was totally minimalist and neat as a pin. Needless to say, the roommate put in for a transfer and was eventually given a single.

Well, good to his word, Munchy hit the club and played and played and played. Day and night, day and night, and day and night again...and again...and again. He played for five straight days and nights with no sleep. Five days of boozing hard until last call at 2 a.m., then shakily facing that horrible four-hour gap until 6 a.m. when the bar opened again. Four long hours of subsisting on nothing but light coffee and the free cookies and orange juice that they passed out to the players on bright orange cafeteria trays, just so no one dropped dead from hypoglycemia. Cookies and juice, like you were a grade school kid playing with your friends in your mom's basement, until finally 6 o-clock rolled back around and you could order that first beer of the day. A beer that was invariably warm, as it had just been stocked. Ahh, sweet memories...but I digress....

On the morning of day six, after more than 120 hours with no sleep, Munchy was in the bathroom urinating when his body finally couldn't take any more. He passed out mid-stream and hit his head on the hard porcelain of the urinal as he went down. Munchy being Munchy, and the Normandie being the Normandie, we pretty much knew all the employees on a first-name basis—no big scene ensued. In fact, the staff took it in stride, like this sort of thing happened all the time. A burly security guard simply picked him up and carried him out to his Bug in the parking lot. He casually tucked Munchy into the driver's seat, threw a blanket on him, and put him down for a well-earned nap. A floorman gathered Munchy's chips and kept them in a rack in the cage, nice and safe. No worries. All good.

No worries indeed, except that when Munchy awoke fourteen hours later, he not only had a nice lump on his forehead, but also a deep red sunburn all over his face from where the sun had shone brightly through the windshield as he slumbered. He looked like a skinny little man-child with a bright red and plump plum head, topped by an unkempt and unwashed shock of blonde hair. His head looked like a deformed and bruised cherry tomato that someone had inadvertently adorned with a dirty blonde wig. His injuries were impossible not to notice and ridiculous to observe.

I know because I watched all of this unfold firsthand. I wasn't there for the entire week-long session; I had come and gone several times during the course of the marathon for a variety of reasons, but I happened to return on the day that he went down and I watched in abject fascination as the security guard cradled him like a baby and gently transported him out of the club like he was an unconscious, male version of Debra Winger at the end of *An Officer and a Gentleman*—sans Richard Gere's Navy cap.

I certainly couldn't leave him alone at that point, so I stayed and played all through his extended nap in the Bug, and I was still playing when I witnessed nothing less than the second coming of Christ. Or rather, the second coming of Munchy.

By the same unholy light that shone down on the cracked and uneven detritus-ridden asphalt of the parking lot, the same harsh and penetrating Southern California light that had burned his pea head bright red, he had somehow been resurrected. I was embroiled in a fairly heated four-to-eight-dollar Hold'em hand when the front doors flew open and there was Munchy, having emerged from his VW death slumber Lazarus-like, looking worse for the wear and quite crimson but astonishingly vertical, if staggering a bit. His body met the floor at an angle of less than ninety degrees, granted, and his trajectory was far from straight and even, but still, he was alive and moving.

Now one might think that this type of experience would trigger some sort of wake-up call for the individual in question. One might presume that perhaps it could be taken as a rock-bottom-type moment and that the subject might take this opportunity to reevaluate his or her lifestyle and make some adjustments. Well, if that's what one might think or presume, then one would be wrong, as one evidently did not fully comprehend the complex, impish idiocy that was Munchy.

Any sane person would have hidden out with no human contact for as long as it took for the facial abnormalities to heal. Not Munchy. Rather than being ashamed of his appearance, he pranced around like a freshly brushed show horse. Instead of crawling into his cave and licking his wounds, Munchy crawled out of the Bug, stood up, stretched, and strolled right back into the club. He proudly retrieved his chips, tossed a few thank-you tokes to those who had helped him, and sat right back down at a three-to-six-dollar Hold'em table, easy as you please.

And I'll be good goddamned if a day and a half later he didn't hit a bad beat jackpot for eight grand. I kid you not. He did it. Just like he said he would. He somehow managed to lose aces full of queens to four aces with a king kicker, which just barely fulfilled the requirements, and he got paid. That was all it took. By losing, he won, ironically enough. And it only cost him a week of his life, a serious head injury, and a third-degree sunburn. Absolute pandemonium broke loose at that point. It was like he had just won the Indy 500, at least among our constituents. There was screaming, cheering, jumping around, hugging, kissing, drink spilling, chairs being knocked over, and carrying on like you wouldn't believe. Things got a little out of hand, to be perfectly frank, as everyone there knew him and his plan, and they all thought it was incredible and cute that he had pulled it off. Still, despite the excess hoopla, which may have been a tad extreme, it was quite a victory. There was no denying it. The little fucker had done it. It was unbelievable, really.

He actually owed me a couple thousand and change at the time and of course made every excuse in the world to try to not pay me back. He offered me different incremental percentages of the total debt, he offered to pay me a certain amount a week for a certain number of weeks, etc. Standard junkie stuff. But after an hour or so of heated debate, he did indeed finally repay me in full, which was like me hitting a jackpot as well. Munchy paying me back—clearing his total debt all at once—was actually a longer shot for me than him hitting his bad beat jackpot. It was like a goddamned biblical miracle had occurred. We had both hit million-to-one shots simultaneously, and these wins required celebration. Therefore, at this point, we took a rare break from the tables, drove over to the Santa Monica Mall, and celebrated this unlikely turn of events by doing some shopping. We eventually returned to the Malibu campus triumphant, if a little banged-up, carrying a dozen bags from Macy's and draped in fancy new Polo threads.

CHAPTER 6

THE BLUFF

AT THE EXACT SAME TIME that I was living in Hermosa Beach, playing Hold'em for a living, listening to Elton on repeat, and writing my *Shell Game* screenplay in 1995, our old friend Munchy was a full-fledged casino kid and had been for several years.

This was four years after I had graduated from Pepperdine in 1991. Following an extended visit to Key West, Florida and a couple of other cross-country oat-sowing excursions, I had returned to the Los Angeles beach community known as the South Bay and set to work trying to jumpstart my writing career by pounding out a poker movie.

Munchy never graduated from Pepperdine. He made it maybe two years or so, but that was it. I forget whether it was due to lackluster grades or gambling away his student loan money (perhaps some combination of both,) but he wound up not being allowed back, at which point Munchy became fully immersed in and committed to *The Life*.

Following his premature departure from school, Munchy started spending just about all of his time at the Normandie Club. So much so, in fact, that at some point he decided to face the inevitable and actually became a professional poker dealer. And yes, he dealt at Normandie. Where else? Again, one could argue it was all my fault...or partly, at least.

He parlayed that position into a floorman gig, first at Normandie, then at the Hollywood Park Casino in Inglewood that was adjacent to the famous Hollywood Park Racetrack. A floorman, or floorwoman, at a card club is like a pit boss, assisting and keeping watch over the dealers, making sure the rotation is going along as it should, seating players, ruling on controversial decisions, deciding when to start new games, and generally keeping tabs on everything happening in their assigned area.

The Hollywood Park gig was a major coup for Munchy. I don't know how he did it, as he was the least responsible individual I had ever known, not to mention that he had just recently been mired in a sticky situation with some rather unsavory individuals—the same sticky situation that had required him to hide out in the motels, don the vest, and carry the heater. Munchy was in debt to the Juice Man to the tune of many thousands of dollars. This was a debt that had grown as Munchy continued to play Hold'em and continued to lose. The more he lost, the more he wanted to get even, hence, the more he borrowed. It was a vicious cycle, but one Munchy did not have a monopoly on; it happens all the time to all kinds of folks.

He never told me the exact figure, but from what I gathered from his demeanor, Munchy's debt was a big number. Once it had gotten so large that Munchy was no longer able to pay the juice—the interest accrued on the loan, an astonishing *5 percent a week*—he was forced to hide out. But Munchy was a good talker. Through his motor-mouth gift for gab, he eventually managed to extricate himself from trouble with the goons and make some sort of deal for them to leave him alone. I suppose they agreed to a payment plan or something. Whatever the details, he was finally allowed to go to work without having to look over his shoulder. He managed to obtain that ever-elusive daydream of "going straight," or as straight as Munchy could go. It was there at Hollywood Park during his time as a floorman that Munchy and I reconnected.

I was playing in the twenty-to-forty-dollar-limit Hold'em game at Hollywood Park just about every day in between writing *The Shell Game* and the occasional beach volleyball game. Imagine my surprise the day I walked in and saw Munchy strutting around the floor with his hair slicked back, draped in a baggy, tan floorman's jacket that was at least two sizes too big. I just about fell over. And there was more. While still working at the Normandie Club, he had evidently met and married a Panamanian Pai Gow dealer named Jo-jo, and they now had three young children together, as well as a fourth that she already had from a previous relationship. Munchy, little, maniac, baby-faced screwball Munchy, was now a hot-shot poker-room floorman with a wife and four kids. Go figure.

Munchy and I shared a few meals and caught up on things, and it was during this time of reconnection that I informed him I was writing a screenplay about card clubs and Hold'em, how I'd had a crazy dream that I could sort of introduce the game to the world. Back then no one outside of the clubs had heard of it. He loved the idea and helped me out with my research here and there. He clarified details for me, like exactly how much the real Juice Man charged in interest on his loans.

It was a good time; I was riding a high and beautiful wave. For a while. Sadly, my career as a professional poker player was about to come to an abrupt end.

My illustrious professional poker career experienced its brutal and ignominious demise one dreadful night about eight months after it began. It was very late at Hollywood Park. I had been having a bad night and had played so long that the last twenty-to-forty-dollar game broke, meaning there weren't enough players left to keep it going. At that point, I made a classic amateur blunder and jumped into a forty-to-eighty-dollar game, which was well out of my bankroll range, a bankroll that had already been depleted.

It wasn't the first time I had played forty-to-eighty dollar. Just a week or so earlier, I had tried it out for the first time. In a staggering case of beginner's luck, I went on a mad rush and won around seven grand in just a few hours. The pretty blonde dealer who dealt my rush said she liked my hemp necklace, bought me a beer, and gave me her phone number. She later visited me at the beach, and we had a lovely, lovely time together. Twice. Score one for ole Sasqy…. That was a pretty good night. This night, however, my second attempt at conquering that same table would not turn out so well.

I played forty-to-eighty-dollar for an hour or two and then *that* game broke. Now here is where I should have gone home. It was four in the morning. I had been playing all day and night, and I had been losing. I was tired and possibly even "on tilt" as they say in the game, meaning I had lost my ever-loving mind and was no longer making rational decisions. Genius that I was, I decided to move to the only Limit Hold'em game still going, which was $80–$160. This was not a smart move, to put it mildly. This was 400 percent out of my bankroll range on any given night and even more so this night, as my roll had already been whacked in half. I had never played in a game that big before, and this was certainly not the time to start. But you know I did it anyway. Munchy, it turned out, didn't have the market cornered on making questionable decisions.

I was already running bad prior to moving to this crazy game, and, of course, I continued to run bad. At one point, I lost a $4,000 pot with a king-high flush to an ace-high flush with just three of the suit on the board. This was a hand that, under normal circumstances, I should have won. To add insult to injury, a few hands later I got outplayed. Not only did I get outplayed, but the outplaying was perpetrated by a loud, obnoxious, fidgety, diminutive Vietnamese gentleman with long rock 'n' roll hair and round, purple-lensed

John Lennon sunglasses. This guy made Munchy look calm and steady. He never stopped talking, called everybody "baby," male or female, and annoyed the hell out of me and everyone else at the table.

One hand, I had king/queen, flopped a king as top pair, bet out eighty dollars, and everybody folded but him. He called. The turn came an ace. I checked, and he quickly bet $160 (too quickly, I thought). I immediately raised to $320, strong and unafraid. I was not worried in the slightest that this loose nut could have the ace, figuring he was attempting to scare me off my pot. He was bluffing, I assumed. Quick as a wink, before I even got my chips fully in the pot, he re-raised to $480. As he did so, the chips were expelled out of his hand as if by a machine. They landed perfectly formed on the felt in four precisely aligned stacks, so fast I barely saw it happen. He was like a sleight-of-hand magician.

He was strongly projecting that he had indeed caught the ace, and I was so out of my element, so tired, and so unused to making or calling bets of that size, I believed the little bugger and folded. He immediately turned over pocket fives. As he exposed them, he declared in a piercing voice, "I bluff you! I bluff you! Pair five! Pair five!" Then he tossed out a "yeah baby" for effect and laughingly raked in my chips.

It wasn't that big of a pot, and it wasn't the one that broke me. I continued to run bad until I only had a couple grand left to my name and had to bail out, but that particular hand stuck with me. I had until then considered myself to be the greatest poker player in the world. If that's a mild exaggeration, let's just say I had a fairly high opinion of my abilities. I was a winning player, more or less, if only on a fairly low level. But after that night and that hand, I thought, *Fuck me. If that little, obnoxious dude who dresses like he's about to go on stage with a Led Zeppelin tribute band can outplay me so easily, I must not be as good as I thought.* It rocked me to my core—hard enough to where I quit. That night. My career as a poker "pro" was over. And while I would eventually, years later, continue to play regularly in casual games and tournaments in Vegas and locally, I never played for a living again.

As some of you who are familiar with the poker world have probably already guessed—and what I was totally oblivious to that night—was that the annoying little Vietnamese dude with the long hair and round shades calling everybody "baby" was actually a guy named Scotty Nguyen. I only found this out because the next time I saw his face years later, it was on the cover of *Poker Digest*, the very same magazine for which, I, at the time, ironically enough, was writing a bimonthly column under the byline *Chip Stax*. In fact, an installment of my column appeared in the very same issue that had his face on the cover. He was on the cover because he had just won the main event of the 1998 World Series of Poker. I kid you not. He had taken first place in the main event of the biggest, most prestigious poker tournament on the planet. Winning the main event of the WSOP for a poker player was like winning the Super Bowl, the World Series, and the heavyweight boxing title combined. It turned out that Scotty was one of the top pros in the world who, just by dumb luck, happened to be killing time at the Hollywood Park $80–$160-limit Hold'em table on that particular night. I must say, as I stared in disbelief at the cover, I did feel a slight pang of comprehension. "Ohhhh," I said to myself. "No wonder…"

CHAPTER 7

THE CALL

THE WAY I CAME TO believe that Harvey Weinstein had stolen my screenplay, while emotionally dramatic, was really quite ordinary. If this was a movie, they would probably have my character walking down the street, spying a movie poster at a bus stop, being struck dead in my tracks, and almost getting run over by a skateboarder. Or I'd be driving in my car stopped at a light, and I'd see a billboard advertising the movie that would so captivate my attention that I would continue to stare at it even after the light had turned green so that the cars behind me would be forced to honk their horns to get me moving. In reality, however, it was a simple phone call from Munchy, although I didn't even know it was Munchy on the line at first.

This was the spring of 1998, seven years after I had graduated from Pepperdine and four or five after Munchy had managed to extract himself from his loan shark troubles and turn his life around, although he was no longer working at Hollywood Park.

It started out a routine day like any other. I was hard at work in my fluorescent-lit editorial office, one of a hundred or so similar offices, housed in a nondescript office building in Pasadena. I was going over the layout for that day's issue of the British tabloid-inspired webzine that I was in charge of writing and editing on a daily basis when my old silver flip phone rang.

The voice on the other end said, "Dude, where are you right now?"

I replied, "Uh, I'm at work in my office."

Then the voice said, "Go to your computer right now and get online. They stole your fucking movie!"

I hadn't spoken to Munchy in quite a while—at least a year, if not more–and our lives had taken separate paths, as is known to happen, so it took me a minute to figure out who I was talking to. He was so excited to get his message out that he hadn't taken the time to identify himself. Concurrently, I was so stunned by what he was saying, I hadn't bothered to ask.

Taken aback as I was, I did as I was told. I sat down at my workstation and followed the instructions the voice provided. I opened up my browser and dialed into the Miramax promotional website I was told to go to, and bam! Smacking me right in the face like a pixilated frying pan was a photograph that I quickly realized was a movie poster that looked very familiar. Not familiar because I had seen it before, but familiar because it looked exactly like the movie poster for my *Shell Game* movie. Or rather, it looked exactly like the poster that would have been printed for my *Shell Game* movie had my script been produced. The poster depicted two guys and a girl, all college-aged. It had a dark, edgy feel to it, and the film it advertised was obviously about poker. Keep in mind that prior to *Rounders*, there hadn't been a poker movie let loose into the culture for a very long time. The genre (or sub-genre) was long since dead and buried. That was one of the goals I'd had in mind and stated out loud when I started to write *The Shell Game*—to resurrect it. I loved poker movies, the few that there were—*The Cincinnati Kid*, *California Split*, that great scene in *The Sting*—and I figured it was about time for another one, one based on my own personal experiences in a more modern world where Texas Hold'em was the star.

Suddenly, out of the corner of my eye, like one spies the imagined fleeting figment of a long-lost friend drifting through a raucous carnival crowd, I noticed the tagline on the poster, which read, "*Trust everyone, but always cut the cards,*" at which point the hair on the back of my neck stood up, and I felt a strange feeling wash over me. I slowly and cautiously read the copy describing the film, and it only took me about three seconds to realize that it was as if they had stolen my script, re-written it, and turned it into this *Rounders* flick. This was just my first moment of awareness—the Big Bang spark of recognition. I hadn't yet come to the stunning realization that the copy I was reading was giving me such a strange feeling because it read like a near verbatim reiteration of the one-page synopsis I had included with each *Shell Game* script I sent out. Could they have had the unmitigated gall to use my own synopsis in their marketing materials? If so, these people were not only stone-cold plagiaristic criminals, but they obviously had no shame whatsoever. However, I had not even realized they had done that yet when I became convinced they had stolen my script. That's how blatantly obvious it seemed to me. I hadn't even read the copy yet and I knew. I knew instantly. I knew from the fucking poster.

What I didn't know was how these Miramax jamokeys had gotten their hands on my screenplay. But whether I knew how they had gotten ahold of it or not, I felt they indeed *had* somehow gotten ahold of it. That much seemed perfectly clear. At that moment, I believed they had read it, ingested it, and regurgitated it into this *Rounders*. The only question that remained was what was I going to do about it?

FROM THE MIRAMAX *ROUNDERS* PROMOTIONAL WEBSITE:

"Rounders is the tale of **(1) Mike McDermott,** *a* **(2) master card player** *who* **(3) trades the** *poker-playing rounds for* **(4) law school** *and a* **(5) shot at a new life** *with his girlfriend Jo. For Mike, the new life he's staking out seems like a legitimate road to success, but it's short on the* **(6) thrills and excitement of back room poker games.** *But when Mike's longtime friend Worm is released from prison, Mike is faced with the high-stakes dilemma of his life: to keep on*

the (7) **straight and narrow** *or deal himself back into the world of the rounders."*

FROM *THE SHELL GAME* SYNOPSIS:

"The Shell Game is a story about money and the people who want it. Choosing to (3) **forsake** *the* (7) **straight and narrow path** *for the* (6) **exciting but unpredictable world of card clubs,** (1) **Jack Baker,** *a* (2) **gifted** *but irresponsible* (4) **college student,** *finds himself cornered by his own recklessness and decides to take a desperate* (5) **shot at instant salvation."**

The annotated numbers are my own addition, but the text is verbatim. I placed the numbers there so that one may, if one so chooses, use them to demonstrate just how similar these two passages really are. Line them up in order, just for fun, should you have the time and inclination. Oh hell, I'll do it for you. That's just the kind of guy I am.

FROM THE MIRAMAX *ROUNDERS* PROMOTIONAL WEBSITE:

Mike McDermott / master card player / law school / trades the / straight and narrow / shot at a new life / thrills and excitement of back-room poker games.

FROM *THE SHELL GAME* SYNOPSIS:

Jack Baker / gifted / college student / forsake the straight and narrow path / shot at instant salvation / exciting but unpredictable world of card clubs.

How's that for a side-by-side comparison? I really don't see how they could possibly be any closer without being identical.

CHAPTER 8

THE ACE

FOLLOWING MY SUDDEN AND VIOLENT ascension to the ceiling of my Pasadena editorial office upon viewing the *Rounders* promotional website, beet red in the face with clouds of hot steam emitting from my ears, I figured the next thing I had better do was get myself a lawyer. I certainly wasn't going to sit still and do nothing. I believed I'd been ripped off and violated in such a blatant fashion that it was difficult to even comprehend. And I hadn't even seen the movie yet. Once *Rounders* was released and I had an opportunity to view it, a whole other level of culpability would surface like an ugly and duplicitous, poker-playing swamp monster. But I wasn't going to wait for that. I already felt they were guilty as sin, and I wasn't going to take it lying down. Legal action seemed like the only available recourse, so I set out to retain myself some counsel.

I made a few attempts on my own, all of which resulted in failure. Every lawyer I spoke to demanded a five- or ten-thousand dollar retainer to even listen to my story. This was money I did not have. Months went by, and I was still without representation. Things were looking bleak, and I started to realize that this was most likely the reason these suckers figured they could steal my story. They knew that I would need a whole bunch of dough to retain a lawyer and a bunch more to keep the case going, and they probably figured—correctly, it turned out—that I couldn't afford the cost.

November of 1998 came, and *Rounders* was released. I went and saw it, of course, and upon my viewing it in the theater, I was more livid than ever. I couldn't believe that not only did it appear as if they had stolen my story but that they had stolen so much of it and in such an obvious and egregious fashion. I was astonished that they had not changed more of the details. It was like they were thumbing their noses at me, daring me to do something about it. There were characters, settings, scenes, and even names that were virtually identical. I can't even explain what a surreal experience it is to be sitting alone in a Pasadena movie theater munching on popcorn, watching what felt like my story flash across the screen thirty feet high in Technicolor. It felt like God was playing some sort of horrible cosmic joke on me.

Funnily enough, either due to budgetary constraints, artistic choices, or both—or perhaps just because they knew they had to change it at least a little bit—they hadn't used all of my screenplay. From my perspective, they seemed to have used approximately the first third or so and stretched that part out into its own story. In *Rounders*, the protagonist, Mike McDermott, portrayed by Matt Damon, sets out for Las Vegas to play in the World Series of Poker at the end of the film. In *Shell Game*, the protagonist, Jack Baker, actually goes to Vegas for the World Series of Poker tournament. Mayhem and shenanigans ensue. Jack Baker. Mike McDermott. That's a lot of hard "k" sounds. Not to mention, in both stories, theirs and mine, the protagonist has a disapproving, pretty blonde girlfriend. Theirs is named Jo. Mine is named Jill. No fooling. Mike and Jack. Jo and Jill. The stupid names even sound alike.

Seems a little bit odd, right? That's not all. Are you ready for this one? Both scripts actually have a character named "Worm." The Edward Norton character in *Rounders* is called "Worm," and I have a character in *The Shell Game* called Klaus Wermer, aka "The Worm." I kid you not. Worm and Worm. Can you freaking believe that? What are the odds? Coincidence? Suffice it to say, when the credits rolled after my second viewing of the film, which I have to admit was fairly entertaining and pretty well done, I stomped angrily out of the theater, resolute in my determination to get myself a lawyer.

As luck would have it, after I started to get serious and put the word out to everyone I had ever met—the ones who thought I was crazy and otherwise—informing them of my situation, I was eventually referred to a guy named John Marder by an attorney named Rose, who happened to be the girlfriend of Chopper, my old roommate from the Manhattan Ave. house in Hermosa where I had written the screenplay. This Marder was alleged to be a heavy hitter who practiced in exactly the specialty I needed.

Marder was an intellectual property attorney working in Los Angeles as part of the firm Manning Marder & Wolfe, at which he was a partner. This was a big break for me. This guy was actually willing to meet me, and I was going to be ready. I needed help. There was nothing I could do on my own, and I knew that something must be done. I needed a shark. I needed a hammer. I needed a hammerhead shark. Something along those lines. And I was willing to do my part. I wasn't going to show up empty-handed like a slacker doofus. I did my homework. I had something real and tangible to present, if given the chance.

An appointment was set for an interview, and I showed up amidst the cavernous, sun-smashed, vertical block architecture of downtown LA at the appointed time. I was armed with a seven-page document I had whipped up for the occasion, along with a righteous helping of moral indignation, a red guitar, three chords, and the truth (minus the guitar and chords).

Following my two painful viewings of *Rounders*, I'd gone home and drawn up a detailed, bullet-pointed, seven-page list of similarities between the movie and my script. I figured Marder may need some convincing. This document was my secret weapon.

The law offices were located high up in the Wells Fargo tower, which was the second tallest building in LA at the time, and the spaces were as polished and fancy as any I had ever seen. It was all very stylish and modern—a luxurious legal bastion of white marble, clean glass, and shiny chrome. As an added embellishment, there were large fish tanks scattered about that housed, naturally, little leopard sharks. Ill-conceived oceanic attorney humor aside, it was all quite slick, fashionable, and opulent. Now I'm not someone who normally rattles easily, nor am I quick to be impressed. However, I must admit, I was a little bit overwhelmed trying to take it all in as I was led by a total knockout of a female assistant in a thousand-dollar dress across several acres of gleaming white marble back to Marder's office.

Marder's private sanctum was even more impressive than the rest of the place. For starters, the room was octagonal with walls that were floor-to-ceiling glass. It felt almost like you were standing in a giant designer fish tank—only this one was, thankfully, not filled with salt water and housed only one land shark. It did come equipped with stunning views of surrounding Los Angeles in all directions. On a clear day, as Marder was quick to inform me, you could even see the Pacific Ocean. From downtown LA. Quite a feat.

So startling was the setting, in fact, that as soon as I walked in, I experienced a little dose of vertigo and almost lost my balance. I was all slanted and sideways and "whoaaah," which isn't like me. Normally, I'm straight as a telephone pole and wholly unflappable. Ask anyone. But this situation was different. I was breathing high and expensive air, and I wasn't used to it. Despite the heavily oxygenated environment, however, I quickly recovered and did not fall. Sasquatches don't go down. Never. If they do, you don't want to be anywhere near there, this much I can assure you. But they don't, so you don't have anything to worry about.

The decor was equally intriguing. There was a pair of authentic, full-sized Samurai swords hanging on the wall behind his desk. In addition to the swords, there were scary-looking antique tribal masks, plated armor, painted shields, hand-hewn spears, and other such ancient warrior type antique accouterments. This guy wasn't kidding around. Marder had gone full throttle with this setup. It was an office meant to intimidate, and it did the trick. It was like being in an octagonal, glass-walled wing of an exclusive museum devoted to tribal warfare in the medieval Far East.

"Who's your decorator?" I inquired, quoting *Caddyshack*. "Benihana?"

I'm not sure if I actually said that out loud. Probably not, but that is certainly what I was thinking. I was also thinking that this was the right guy for the job. This guy was a fighter, a competitor. I could tell right away that he did not like to lose and probably didn't very often. For instance, he was quick to inform me that he was a black belt in karate. Of course he was. I was in love. I was like a walking and talking version of one of those emojis with the heart eyes. This Marder was my guy. No doubt about it. Now all I had to do was convince him to take the case. For free.

After the introductions were made and the obligatory small-talk about what a sublime office setting he had created subsided, he sat me down, and another great-looking assistant brought me a bottle of Perrier. I didn't ask for it, mind you, but she brought it anyway. I don't even drink Perrier—too snooty for my taste. But I sure as heck did on that day.

As we settled in, I prepared to launch into my pitch. The moment of truth was upon us. Thrown as I might have been by the posh and aggressive atmosphere, I'm no wilting flower, and I was determined. I had a fire in my gut and a righteous cause to promote. I was ready for action, and I was armed. I had my .45 caliber, seven-page document of similarities cocked and loaded, and it was powerful. There was no doubt about it. However, wouldn't you know it? Before I was even able to utter one word about my situation, before I was able to unsheathe my document and wield it like the mighty Samurai sword I knew it was (not to mix weaponry metaphors), before a single syllable escaped my Perrier-moistened lips, Marder took the lead and launched into a lengthy diatribe as to why I had no case. I never even got a single word out. He just rolled right over me like a well-dressed and coiffed steamroller of negativity. It threw me for a loop, let me tell you.

"Let me explain to you how it is," he started. "Everyone thinks they've had an idea stolen from them at one time or another. It's a psychological trick. It's all ego related. These are all fantasies. It's a bit of cerebral chicanery…. There are only five different plotlines in fiction. Five. That's it."

Five? I thought to myself, taking a sip of Perrier. *Damn. That's not many.*

He went on. "Every story you've ever read, every movie you've ever seen, are all derivative of these five basic plotlines. *The Wizard of Oz, Star Wars, Rocky, Gone with the Wind*...they're all essentially the same story. The mind tricks us. When we have an idea we think is original, it's not really original at all. I've talked to dozens of people, hundreds even, who claim their ideas were stolen and turned into this movie or that movie, but it's all nonsense. And beyond that, it's very difficult to prove in court. Very difficult. Unless it's a verbatim reiteration, which it never is...."

Here he paused and seemed to soften just a hair.

"I'm not saying it doesn't ever happen. It does, on rare occasions. I argue intellectual property cases. That's my specialty. For example, Greg Kinnear is a close personal friend of mine, and I recently won a case for him. He had an idea for a TV show that was rejected by the producers he met with, but then they used it anyway. And it turned out to be a hit show. But he's the exception, not the rule. The odds you actually have a case are a million to one. A million to one. I'm sorry. But I'm glad to meet you and take the meeting. How's your Perrier?"

"Uh, it's great. Thanks," I replied, my head spinning.

But he wasn't quite done with me.

"You said on the phone that you never met directly with anyone from Miramax. Is that correct?"

"Yes," I confirmed.

"And you never spoke with or communicated with anyone from Miramax or any of the producers or writers of *Rounders*..."

"No."

"Okay. So they will validate your parking at the receptionist desk. It was a pleasure to meet you."

That was it. He was done. He had said his piece. He had met with me as agreed, made up his mind without hearing a single word of my pitch, and that was that. It was over before it started. I was in a state of shock. I wasn't even sure what had just happened. Marder, eager to be done with me and move on to the next thing on his agenda, stood up to shake my hand goodbye. But somehow, even in my bewildered state, instead of taking his hand, I instinctively handed him the manila envelope that had been burning a hole in my lap since I sat down.

"What's this?" he asked.

"It's a list I compiled of all the similarities between my screenplay and the *Rounders* movie. It's seven pages long. Bullet-pointed."

His curiosity being at least mildly piqued, he opened the envelope and removed the document. Then he sat back down and perused it. His expression changed immediately as he read things like...

- Both films are set in the little-known subculture of high-stakes poker and poker clubs.

- Both films revolve around the specific game of Texas Hold'em.

- This is the first time in the history of movies that Texas Hold'em has been featured in a film.

- In both films, Texas Hold'em interferes with the protagonist's studies and relationships, causes him physical violence, and threatens his life.

- In both films, the protagonist chooses poker over academia.

- In both films, the protagonist loses his tuition money gambling.

- Both movies have a character named "Worm," which is not a common nickname, and I have never met a poker player by that nickname.

- Worm, the best friend in *Rounders*, has the ace of spades tattooed on his arm. In *The Shell Game*, Jack has an ace of spades etched on his Zippo lighter.

- In both films, the protagonist loses all the money he has in the world in one hand of Texas Hold'em.

- In both films, in the hand where all the money he has in the world is lost, the protagonist goes "all in" with a full house and loses to a larger full house. Mike loses nines full of aces to aces full of nines (*Rounders*). Jack loses jacks full of aces to aces full of jacks (*The Shell Game*).

- In both films, the girlfriend is neglected for the poker table and voices her disappointment at the neglect.

- At one point in *Rounders*, Mike explains to the audience the rudimentary fundamentals of Texas Hold'em and some of the strategy.

- At one point in *The Shell Game*, Jack explains to Munchy and the audience the rudimentary fundamentals of Texas Hold'em and some of the strategy.

- *Rounders* has a scene where Mike tells his professor which hands are the "premium" starting hands.

- *The Shell Game* has a scene where Jack explains to Munchy which hands are the "premium" starting hands.

- *Rounders* has a sexy female card club employee who comes over to Mike's house, kisses him, and offers him sex while Jo is away.

- *The Shell Game* has a sexy female card club employee who comes over to Jack's house, kisses him, and offers him sex while Jill is away.

- In *Rounders*, Jo finds a wad of cash in Mike's pants that makes a liar out of him and gets him in big trouble.

- In *The Shell Game*, Jill finds a wad of cash in Jack's desk that makes a liar out of him and gets him in big trouble.

That's just a taste. (For the complete list, see "Extra Bullet One.")

Now I'm no mind reader, but if I had to guess, right about now you might be saying to yourself, "Wow. That is a fuck-ton of similarities, and it's not even the complete list.... I wonder if this has ever happened to anybody else?"

The answer is a resounding "yes." It happens all the time. Maybe a little bit less now than it used to because of my case and the change to the law, but it for sure still happens and has happened a zillion times.

When I first came to believe that they had stolen my *Shell Game* script, I reached out to a former neighbor of mine from Willimantic. Upon graduating from UCONN, Carol managed to land a job with a large production company in New York. When I emailed her and explained what I thought had happened with my script, her response was surprisingly swift and somewhat shocking.

"Not only am I sure that they stole your script," she said succinctly, "but they do it all the time. Every day. Everybody knows it. It's common knowledge on the street here."

No kidding, I thought to myself. *Figures.*

The Art Buchwald case comes to mind. Art was a famous American writer and humorist, and at one point in his career, he penned a movie treatment for Paramount Pictures called *King for A Day*. According to Wikipedia, his pitch was as follows:

> *"A rich, educated, arrogant, extravagant, despotic African potentate comes to America for a state visit. After being taken on a grand tour of the United States, the potentate arrives at the White House. A gaffe in remarks made by the President infuriates the African leader. His sexual desires are rebuffed by a black woman State Department officer assigned to him. She is requested by the President to continue to serve as the potentate's United States escort. While in the United States, the potentate is deposed, deserted by his entourage and left*

destitute. He ends up in the Washington ghetto, is stripped of his clothes, and befriended by a black lady. The potentate experiences a number of incidents in the ghetto and obtains employment as a waiter. In order to avoid extradition, he marries the black lady who befriended him, becomes the emperor of the ghetto, and lives happily ever after."

I don't know how deep your knowledge of movies goes, but if this reminds you of the Eddie Murphy classic *Coming to America*, congrats. You are correct. The only problem was that a few years after Art wrote his treatment, when *Coming to America* was shot and released, the story was credited solely to Eddie Murphy. Buchwald's name was nowhere to be found. Nor was he compensated. Buchwald sued, won, and later settled for $900,000. Not bad, Art. Well done.

Then there's the story of the Tom Cruise movie *The Last Samurai*. Two brothers, Aaron and Matthew Benay, claimed that their script, which was also coincidentally tilted *The Last Samurai*—and was about an American war veteran who goes to Japan to help the Imperial Army by training it in the methods of modern warfare—was written in the late 1990s, registered with the Writers Guild of America, and their agent, David Phillips, had verbally pitched the story to the eventual producers of the Cruise movie that grossed $350 million worldwide. The judge and jury, however, somehow had doubts that said pitch ever took place, and amazingly, they lost the case.

There are a slew more. I could go on for days, but I think I've made the point. Everything is a dice roll in this life—you just never know what will happen. Even when you know, you don't know. But what I personally wanted to know at the moment was what Marder thought of my own case.

"Is this accurate?" he asked, now visibly agitated, having glanced through my extensive list of similarities.

"Extremely. I was very careful not to overstate anything," I assured him.

"If this is accurate, you have a case," he said emphatically. He had changed his tune entirely. He'd made a complete 180-degree reversal.

"It's accurate as fuck," I confirmed again. I may not have used profanity.

"Wow. This is unbelievable," he said, as he continued scanning through the pages. "I can't believe they thought they could get away with this.... Okay, you've convinced me. If this checks out, I'll take the case on a standard one-third contingency, meaning whatever settlement we receive, you get two-thirds, and the firm receives one-third. You will pay no retainer and no fees, but I will need you to do some of the legwork as we don't have a budget. Is that agreeable to you?"

"Yes," I responded quietly and nodded while screaming inside.

I was nothing short of thrilled. I had done it. I was going to have my day in court. Justice was going to be served.

We were really going to get these bastards. This fucking guy with the octagonal glass-walled office and the shark tanks and the marble and the swords and the masks and the Karate and the supermodel assistants—*this guy* could do it. I had come to the right place. It was all happening. I was elated. But we weren't quite done with the meeting.

"Let me ask you something," Marder continued. "You said you never met with anyone from Miramax. You never spoke to anyone from Miramax or any of the writers or producers of *Rounders*. Not in person or on the phone…"

"No."

"Well, then how did they get their hands on your script? To win these kinds of cases, we need to prove two things: similarity, which you seem to have in spades, and access. We need an access theory. If you never met with them or talked to them, how did they get your screenplay?"

This was a very good question, and one I had pondered myself. I really didn't know. I believed they had gotten it, but I didn't know *how*. I had sent my *Shell Game* script out to multiple studios, networks, and production companies on both coasts, and I was prudent enough to have kept detailed notes on exactly where I'd sent it. I knew where each one had gone. I knew to whom each package was addressed and even which cover letter they had received, as I used different ones. But I had scanned through my notes just prior to this meeting, and Miramax wasn't listed as one of the recipients. It was a puzzler, to be sure. That should tell you something about just how many similarities there were in the two stories and how specific they were. I didn't even know how they got it. I had no *access theory* whatsoever, and yet Marder took the case anyway. On contingency. With no retainer. But not without sending me home with an assignment.

"Go find out how they got it," he instructed me.

So I did.

CHAPTER 9

THE GUN

HAVING FINALLY FOUND MARDER, MY lawyer, my guy—the sharp ace who was going to fight like an armor-suited wolverine against these sons-o-bitches who I believed had stolen my screenplay—I was feeling good and strong. I left Marder's fancy pants offices walking on air. I was thrilled that I now had this legal ninja on my side. This was a dude who obviously had the training, expertise, experience, and resources that I needed to make my case and win.

I wasn't greedy. I just wanted what was fair. More than money, even, what I really would have liked was the credit. I'd much rather not have had to sue anybody. I'm not a litigious person by nature, and I'm not all that fond of lawyers as a breed, as you may have gathered.

If Miramax or the producers or whoever had just called me up and offered me whatever scale was then and a "story by" credit, I would have signed over the rights to my *Shell Game* script in a minute. Sure, I might have been slightly disappointed that they weren't going to film my movie as written, but I was a realist. I knew how things worked. A "story by" credit on that film would have been my ticket into the show. It would have served as a calling card from which I could then book new jobs, which is all I ever wanted. I had other stories to tell.

Unfortunately, the way I saw it, they chose to take the easy way out and steal it, because it was easier and cheaper. And they figured they could get away with it. However, at this point in our journey, we still had no idea how they could have gotten their hands on my script. I did have my own theory, but it was vague.

I had sent the script out to a dozen places on both coasts. The film industry is fairly insular. These guys all know each other. My feeling was that it must have gotten passed from one hand to another until the hand that received it was the hand of someone who worked at or with Miramax. Marder, of course, wanted more than that. He was a lawyer after all, and he was doing his lawyer thing. Courts like details, not vague theories. And I have to admit, I would have loved to find some sort of smoking gun that would explain exactly how they had gotten it without having to rely on theories or conjecture. I would have loved to have solved the riddle, thus giving Marder his access theory on a silver platter.

Given the Lilliputian nature of the shack I was living in and its close proximity to the 210 freeway, which you could hit if you spit over the fence, whenever I returned home, I always felt like I was existing inside a Tom Petty or John Cougar song, and not in a particularly romantic way. But it was close to town, and you could walk to a lot of cool stuff like local burger joints, second-run movie theaters, used bookstores, and some very good, authentic Mexican cantinas. Pasadena is actually a pretty nice place to live, at least for three seasons a year. Summers are brutal.

And so it was that on a particularly clear and cool fair winter day, I set out on my mission to uncover the elusive "access theory" Marder had instructed me to find. Ready to commence my endeavor with a full heart and brave soul, I casually strolled over to the Pasadena Public Library, which was just a mile or so from the two-room shotgun shack where I resided. I entered the beautifully designed and well-appointed building dutifully but not especially optimistically, as I honestly didn't expect to find anything of use. This idea that there was a "smoking gun" of some sort, one that I would be able to uncover during the course of my work as an extremely amateur private investigator, just didn't seem plausible. Nothing was ever that easy. But I was obliged to make a diligent effort, and that's what I was going to do.

I nonchalantly approached the reference desk and asked the friendly, bespectacled older lady sitting there if she happened to have any address books for movie studios. I had with me my notes of where I had sent my script, and even pessimistic as I was that anything fruitful was going to come of this, I was going to give it a go nonetheless.

The reference desk lady happily handed me a thick blue loose-leaf binder. Contained within it were the addresses of every movie studio and production company that happened to be in business at that time. I found this to be awfully convenient, and I thanked her profusely. Nevertheless, as I said, I wasn't overly optimistic that I would find anything of value. The odds were stacked against it. I knew what Marder wanted, and I knew it was important to the case, but I really didn't even know what I was looking for. However, sometimes in life, once in a while, usually when you least expect it, the stars align and things fall neatly into place. As luck would have it, on that fate-filled winter day, sitting quietly in the handsomely appointed confines of the Pasadena Public Library inside that nondescript blue binder, against all odds, I would find the legendary smoking gun. And with it, I would find my salvation. At least for the moment.

It didn't even take very long. I had only been there for a few minutes when I made the discovery that would lead to the ultimate revelation. The first thing I did, of course, was look up the address of Miramax Film Co. They were the ones who had made *Rounders*, so this seemed like the logical place to start. I found it easily enough. It was right there in the book listed as 99 Hudson St., New York, NY.

Okay, so that's where Miramax lived. Now, which one of these places here in my notes is at least in their area? I went down the list and looked up the addresses of a couple of places I had sent my screenplay. No luck. Nothing there. But then suddenly, as if pre-ordained, the tide turned. In my notes, I came across a company called Gotham Entertainment Group. They were one of the places I had sent my script. As soon as I read the name, a little light bulb went off in my head. The more I thought about it, the more I started to remember these Gotham folks. I started to recall that they had a very appealing entry in the *Writer's Market* guidebook that I used to research places to send my screenplay. I recalled that they stood out to me for several reasons, the first one being that they stated categorically, right in their entry in the book, that they accepted unsolicited material. This was, for an aspiring screenwriter in my position, like finding a proverbial Cadillac in a Cracker Jack box, to paraphrase Meatloaf.

The whole "We don't accept unsolicited material" mantra had been the bane of my existence up to that point. "Unsolicited" meaning that the writer in question had no agent, lawyer, or other such representation presenting the material for him or her. It meant that the writer in question was not yet at that stage; they had not been produced and had neither notoriety nor decent contacts of any kind. Virtually every studio, network, and production company had a strict "We do not accept unsolicited material" policy. You had to have an established and well-connected agent, lawyer, or manager submit your work on your behalf, or they wouldn't even look at it. That was the general mandate for most places but not all of them, at least not at that time. Now, of course—some would say thanks to me and my case—it's exponentially harder. Now no one will look at anything, ever.

I recently sent a query letter and a script sample to CAA, a big agency here in Los Angeles, and it came back with a letter stating that they don't read or even open material sent into them, and they never will. And they are an agency, not a studio. Agents are supposed to represent talent. If they refuse to even look at anything, ever, how do they sign new writers? Beats the heck out of me.

But back then there were still gaps in the system, such as the Gotham plan to actually announce that they did indeed accept unsolicited material. HBO was another example. They had read my work and replied, despite the fact that I had no agent. Spelling Entertainment was another, as I had a friend who worked there who was able to place it in the proper pile for me. But these were rare exceptions.

So how does one get to a point where one has been successful enough to garner the attention of legitimate representation if one can't even get anyone to agree to look at their prospective work because they don't have representation? Good question. I have no idea. Hence, you can imagine how excited I was to find these wonderfully open-minded Gotham Entertainment Group folks who seemed to understand my predicament completely.

Also catching my eye, as I once again examined the Gotham Entertainment Group *Writer's Market* entry, having since retrieved the book from the shelf, was the fabulously unexpected line, "*We have a deal with Miramax.*"

"Holy Mother of God," I said out loud. They have a deal with Miramax. I sent them my script. Miramax made *Rounders.* I felt the blood rush to my head, and I sat straight up in my chair. "Whoa," I said to myself. "Marder is going to like this...."

But I wasn't done. I needed to finish the job and make sure I had all my ducks in a row before notifying Marder of this fabulously fortuitous turn of events. So I took the next step. I opened up the blue binder again, and I looked up the address of this Gotham Entertainment Group.

That was the moment that, at least in my mind, the high gothic ceiling of the Pasadena Public Library opened up like the retractable roof of a football stadium and the light and glory of Heaven shone down directly on the table where I was sitting, while an unseen angelic choir sang their most melodic song of glory to the highest. For right there, staring me in the face, plain as day, was the address. It was listed as 99 Hudson Street, New York, NY. The very same address as Miramax.

The ever-elusive smoking gun had been found. The miracle had occurred. Legal Nirvana had been achieved. We now had our access theory. It couldn't be any clearer. I sent it right to them.

I dug a little deeper, and I uncovered more smoking, and more gun to go with it. Gotham Entertainment Group was actually started by Miramax employees. Not only did Gotham and Miramax share the very same address and not only did Miramax have a "first look" deal with Gotham, meaning that Gotham could not move forward with any project of any kind without offering it to Miramax first, but Gotham was also actually a recently launched, brand new company that had been started by Miramax employees. For all intents and purposes, they were the same company. The same entity. Gotham was really just an offshoot of Miramax with offices in the very same building just a couple of floors down.

If one was a cynical type, one could suspect that Gotham was set up purely or at least partially as a clearing house to find new material for their bosses upstairs and that their acceptance of unsolicited scripts would mean that a never-ending stream of story ideas would pour through their transom, ideas that they could plunder at will with very little worry about legal repercussions.

How could they feel so secure? This was due to a one-line philosophy Marder would later teach me as we prepared for court. It was called "*On the likelihood that Plaintiff will not retain counsel.*" What it meant was that since the aspiring screenwriters who were sending Gotham their scripts were likely doing so with no representation or backing of any kind, it made the odds that they would possess the resources and wherewithal to retain a lawyer to sue for infringement very slim. "*On the likelihood that Plaintiff will not retain counsel.*" It sounded like a twisted, evil little motto.

Regardless of their motives for setting it up, it was instantly apparent that these two companies, Gotham and Miramax, were basically the same. Gotham's founder, Patrick McDarrah, the gentleman to whose attention I had addressed my *Shell Game* script, had been the director of Miramax International just prior to moving two floors down and hanging his shingle out as Gotham Entertainment Group. Now he had his "own company" and a first-look deal with his old bosses upstairs. These two companies couldn't be any more closely related if they were two heads on the same body.

Furthermore, as is noted in the court documents, since this first-look deal had been in place, *more than twenty projects* had been passed back and forth between Gotham and Miramax. And this was right around the same time frame in which I had sent them my script. They were literally and figuratively in each other's pockets. There was no denying it; it was an avalanche of access theory. This case was going to be a slam dunk. We were going to win.

CHAPTER 10

THE FLOP

THE FIRST SICKENINGLY PERVERSE TRAVESTY of justice perpetrated by the courts in the *Grosso v. Miramax, Rounders* case occurred early on in the proceedings. It was directly related to the aforementioned long list of similarities between my *Shell Game* script (see Extra Bullet One) and the *Rounders* script that I had compiled.

Upon our filing the first complaint, where the lawyers used my seven-page similarity document in the brief, and after many months and years of waiting, during which time the court was allegedly "reviewing the facts," the decision finally came back: "*No substantial similarities can be found between the two works.*"

The court ruled, right smack in the face of the *seven pages* of specific and airtight similarities, plus the two virtually identical synopses paragraphs, that there weren't substantial similarities that would warrant the case progressing. They dismissed it outright. Right there and then. It was literally unbelievable. No further explanation was given, even though there were indeed substantial similarities, and we had outlined them clearly and precisely. The similarities were actually extremely substantial—extraordinarily substantial, even—and significantly numerous and detailed. Yet that was the court ruling. Somehow. I was dumbfounded. It made no sense. What were they looking at? What weren't they seeing? I had no clue.

Luckily, if you can call it that, Marder, the ace, had an ace up his sleeve. We weren't dead yet. Marder was a fighter, and he wasn't going to give up at the first sign of trouble.

Seemingly just as outraged by the ruling as I was, Marder filed an appeal to this ruling on the grounds that there was an "extra element" present in this particular case. He argued that even though I had never met personally with Miramax, there was a *"breach of implied contract."* He argued that when someone like me mails in a screenplay to a studio, or production house, or what have you, there is an *implied contract* that states that if they decide to use your work, you should be credited and compensated.

This was a brand new idea and a controversial one at that. No one had ventured down this particular legal path before. Marder was breaking new ground, and a lot of folks thought he was crazy, that we had no chance. But his argument evidently made enough sense to the appeals court for them to agree. After many more months and years of waiting—and despite the idiotic "no substantial similarities" ruling—the Court of Appeals for the Ninth Circuit finally ruled that the presence of this "extra element" pre-empted federal copyright law. This caused them to overrule the original dismissal and allow the case to proceed. We were saved. For the moment, anyway. We had fresh hope. And the world took notice.

This was Marder's baby. Instead of charging right up the middle of old-fashioned federal copyright law, he called an audible at the scrimmage line and pitched out a "*breach of implied contract*" tailback sweep for the first down. The appeals court determined that this "extra element" was worth hearing more about, so they kicked the case down to state court for evaluation. This decision was wholly unique and unprecedented, and it actually changed United States copyright law, seemingly in favor of the writers. They actually rewrote the law.

This ruling shook Hollywood right to its seedy foundations. Shockwaves reverberated in all directions. It sent the studios into a full-blown, maniacal, panicked frenzy. Suddenly, *The Hollywood Reporter* and *Variety* were running front page stories on the case. They were followed by CBS, NBC, ABC, the *LA Times*, the *New York Times*, the *Washington Post*, NPR, and just about every other major media outlet you can imagine.

Hundreds upon hundreds of web pages sprung up discussing the issue. All kinds of heavy-hitter hot-shot producers chimed in with their opinions. At one point, all of the Hollywood studios actually joined hands with Miramax to line up against me and this perceived threat to their business. That's how big it was. So big that Marder was named the goddamned *California Lawyer of the Year* for his work in changing the law.

Do you have any idea how many stinking lawyers there are in California? I don't know either, but there's a hell of a lot of them. This I can assure you.

Articles popped up all over the place like mushrooms in a well-fertilized and watered field. Some were angry and defensive in tone, with the author calling me names, accusing me of being a charlatan, etc. while others were supportive, the author happy that the studios were going to finally be held accountable for their actions. I even gave a few interviews, as you saw earlier. Can you imagine? Ole Sasqy.

An interesting side note to all this is how quickly you realize just how inaccurate the reporting in the media actually is, once you become the subject of the story. I'm not saying that there was "fake news" printed or anything along those lines, but they did pretty much always get most of the facts wrong every single time.

One article stated that I had attended Pepperdine Film School when Pepperdine didn't even have a film school. Others misspelled my name, got my age wrong, got the location of my residence wrong, got my history wrong, got my quotes wrong, and got many of the case facts wrong.

People tend to believe what they read in the paper or see on TV or, more relevant to today's culture, look up on the internet. But I'm telling you firsthand, don't believe everything you read. Or maybe anything you read. And I'll tell you why.

I don't care what anyone says. I don't care how many awards a particular media outlet has won or how prestigious said media outlet may be on the global stage. The pure and simple truth is no one is really checking the facts. They're just not. Checking facts doesn't sell papers or get ratings or clicks or make headlines. The people whose job it is to check facts don't want to do it. It's a boring waste of time. They're either too lazy, too busy, or just don't care. Or possibly all three. That is the plain truth. I kid you not.

CHAPTER 11

THE JOKER

I HAVEN'T BEEN IN TOUCH with Munchy for many years. The last time I had any contact with him was when he was deposed for my court case against Miramax. The funny thing about Munchy's deposition was that it didn't go as planned. Instead of him just going on the record with the facts, corroborating my story and being done with it, as any normal person would have done, he decided to take a wide and unexpected Munchy turn into uncharted goofball territory. The little rascal used the opportunity not to help me with my case, which was his sole purpose for being there, but instead to self-aggrandize himself and throw me right under the bus in the process.

Rather than just telling the lawyers that *The Shell Game* screenplay was based on my life, that he was around when I was working on the script and actually witnessed me writing it, Munchy decided to go for a full-on Hail Mary blind-side power grab. It was a long shot, for sure, but Munchy loved long shots. Those were his favorite kinds of wagers.

In the end, he didn't really make much of a negative impact (or any impact). It wasn't like he ruined the case or anything, but instead of just being honest and helpful, Munchy told the lawyers that *he* actually wrote *The Shell Game*, and *he* was responsible for *Rounders*, and *he* was the one who should be suing Miramax and receiving whatever monies and recognition were coming down the line. I guess I shouldn't have been all that surprised. You couldn't necessarily count on Munchy for anything, but you could always count on Munchy to be Munchy. Nonetheless, it did catch me a little off guard. I thought we were friends.

Munchy wasn't working at that time, as far as I knew. The last time I saw him in person, he had been relegated to staying home with his four kids in a Mr. Mom type of situation, which is a fine and noble vocation, and I'm not knocking it. I mention it only because he must have felt particularly bored and isolated at that particular time. "Out of the action," as they say in the game. Then, sure enough, wham-bam out of the blue, he's called to center stage in a fancy office building with lots of important-looking people in suits who all seem to know exactly who he is and all seem genuinely interested in what he has to say. They're doting on him and offering him beverages and treating him like he's special. I guess he just couldn't help himself.

Munchy trying to take credit for writing my script is especially ironic when you consider the fact that Munchy couldn't write. At all. I don't want to sound mean, but for the purposes of reporting the truth of this story, Munchy could barely spell his own name. This is not some bitter opinion of my own invention. Munchy himself, if you asked him to his face, would not argue with this assessment. It wasn't like it was a secret, which is why it's all so perplexing. I'm not saying he was dumb. Not by any means. He was a bright enough guy, to be sure, but he simply could not write. I don't know if he grew up dyslexic or otherwise afflicted, but he could not write a coherent sentence to save his life. How, you may ask, did he even make it through two scant years of college without having to write any papers? Good question. Here's your answer: I wrote them for him. I kid you not. Most of them, anyway. And I was happy to do it. Ungrateful motherfucker. But that's not all. Oh no, it gets better.

Even funnier than that, if you can believe this one, back in 1995, when I was living in Hermosa Beach, playing Hold'em for a living and writing *The Shell Game*, Munchy decided he wanted to go back to school. He had made it through almost two years at Pepperdine before succumbing completely to the siren song of the card room, and he figured that now would be a good time to finish it out. An admirable enough endeavor, granted, but the way he went about it, if you're the judgmental sort, could possibly be considered a bit less than admirable. Admittedly, I was complicit.

At the time, Munchy had Tuesdays off from his day job dealing cards at Hollywood Park, and he was serious enough about this plan that he actually enrolled in one class at the Malibu Pepperdine campus. The class met just once a week on Tuesdays. I can't even remember what the class was, but it was some sort of new age humanities-type deal that required him to take no tests of any kind. His grade would be based solely on the paper that he was required to write each week. One paper per week for twelve weeks. At the end, the professor would average all the grades of all the papers and that would be his grade in the class. No tests, no quizzes—just these papers. This was perfect for Munchy, as it fit squarely into his schedule and didn't require him to do any studying or actually learn anything. The one remaining issue was that pesky weekly paper. Needless to say, Munchy never wrote a single word of any of the twelve papers. Most of the time he didn't even know what they were about. Sometimes I didn't even know what they were about, and I wrote them.

It was the same drill every week. Munchy would pick me up in Hermosa Beach around 10 a.m. on Tuesday morning, and we would drive to Malibu. We always stopped at The Reel Inn on PCH for sushi, beer, and sake on the way in order to mentally prepare ourselves for the hard work that followed. Munchy, God bless him, always picked up the tab. This gratis spread of delights was my "payment" for writing the weekly papers. Let's face it: I worked cheap. Since I was playing Hold'em at Hollywood Park almost every day and still winning consistently at this point, I was flush with all kinds of disposable cash and didn't really need any extra money. I was happy for the ride, the distraction, and of course, the high-quality seafood and cocktails. We would gorge ourselves on sushi, get very drunk on beer and sake, and then Munchy would attempt to pilot his minivan as best he could up the hill onto campus. That was always quite the thrill ride, let me tell you. I'm not sure how we made it any time, let alone every time.

He would take me straight to the computer lab, where he would sit me down and set me on my task of scribing that week's paper. Sometimes I was presented with a question to answer or a general topic to expound upon, and sometimes not. Sometimes Munchy had fallen asleep in class or lost his notes. As a result, he wouldn't have any idea whatsoever as to the topic of the paper. I mean, he had absolutely no idea what "he" was supposed to be writing about. Not even a vague notion. Hard to believe, I know, but it's true. Those days were especially challenging for me for obvious reasons, and I would be sure to imbibe an extra flagon of sake before tackling the assignment just to get the creative juices flowing.

It was on those unknowable, mystery subject days that I was forced to get really creative. I had no other choice. I was under the obligation of producing a paper, and a good one, out of thin air with no topic or guidelines of any kind. I was on a tight deadline. It wasn't like I had a week, or a day, or even half a day to complete the damn thing.

Depending on how long we had lingered at the sushi place, I normally had around half an hour. Thirty minutes. With no topic, no headline, no subject, and no idea where to start or what to do. I was flying completely blind. It was a challenge; I can tell you that. And it wasn't particularly fun. But I did it anyway. Well, occasionally it was a little fun. I would typically finish about two minutes before the class started. This gave Munchy only a small window of time to print the thing out and rush over to the classroom. Sometimes he'd be able to glance through the paper as he walked or skim it quickly before class started, just so he was semi-familiar with it, and sometimes not. Sometimes he barely had enough time to tear apart the perforated sheets and hand it in, totally oblivious to what I had written or what it was about.

Each week the class would discuss each student's paper that had been handed in the week before. This constituted the whole of the class. All they did was read and discuss each student's paper from the previous week. This was some class. Not too complicated. But this was adult education. What could you expect? And yet it was on those days, when the professor wanted to discuss a paper Munchy had handed in the prior week totally unread—a paper Munchy knew absolutely nothing about, a paper that I was unable to even explain to him as I really didn't even know what it was about myself—that Munchy had to get creative as well. And get creative he did.

Munchy normally relayed the details of what had occurred in class to me on the car ride home. I was always curious as to how he had played it off, and I wanted him to get a good grade despite the idiotic nature of the endeavor. What can I say? I take pride in my work.

Munchy would usually keep me in the dark for a while to build the suspense. He was quite the showman. We'd be in his mini-van weaving back down the hill after class had ended, not necessarily in any particular lane but pretty much using all of them, and he'd start off by saying something like, "I got called on in class today. He wanted me to talk about last week's paper."

"Uh-oh," I'd reply, taking the bait. "That's the one where I had no topic and I had to wing it. Did you read it? Did you know what it was about when he called on you?"

"No. Didn't have time."

"Oh, boy. I can't really even remember what it was about myself. I think I was blacked out most of the time I was writing it, but I recall getting a little whacky...."

"Oh, I know. You did. More than a little. I just read it for the first time now after class. I don't understand a word of it. Good thing you work cheap."

"So what did you do?" I'd inquire. "In class? When he called on you?"

"The teacher goes, 'Very interesting paper this week, Rudy. How did you come up with it?'" Munchy's real name was Rudy.

"Oh, boy. How did you?" I'd question. I was curious myself. And I was nervous for him. But it was at times like these when Munchy really shone. He could BS like nobody's business. He was a world champion.

"So I leaned back in my chair," Munchy said, acting it out for me as he's driving, taking up multiple lanes, running over construction cones. "Okay, so I got no idea what it's about or what you did, none—nothing. So I go, 'Well, first I pour myself a little tequila.... Then I squeeze a little twist of lime in it.... Then I let the tequila mix with the lime, and then I take a few sips and I let my mind wander and I sit down at the computer, and it just comes flowing out.'" By now, Munchy was beaming with pride and laughing. Beaming and laughing, while weaving all over the road.

"Holy Christ!" I exclaimed. "He bought that?"

"Yup, totally!" Munchy affirmed, now in hysterics over his own cleverness. "I got a fucking A!" At which point Munchy finally caved and threw the paper at me.

"You mean *I* got an A...." I quickly corrected him as I glanced at the title page that had been scrawled upon in large, cursive lettering with red Sharpie. It read, "*Rudy, I don't know what this has to do with the assignment, but as a funny, intriguing, insightful essay, I give it top marks!!!*" Above this love note, haughtily presiding over the two-dimensional crime scene of verbalized nonsense, was a big, fat red *A*. I couldn't believe it.

"Yeah, sure, well, you, me, we..." Munchy stammered, followed by a final utterance he unleashed from its duplicitous and sinister lair in an extremely clear and concise fashion with no stuttering at all, as tonally sincere in its falseness as it would be if he was expressing a notion as banal as, "It looks like rain." A statement that expressed succinctly, in a perfectly encapsulated and simplistic phrase, all that is wrong with the world today. Or at least a decent part of it.

"My name is on the paper," he said flatly.

His name was on the paper. He had me there. Indeed, it was. And the band played on....

I only bring up this story because that is exactly the same line lovable little Munchy handed my team of lawyers during his deposition. Once they realized that he was going to try to take credit for my script, they were forced to do some damage control. They had to do *something*. Opposing counsel was present and, of course, loving every minute of it. They were drocling like hungry jackals. Flabbergasted and frustrated as they were, in a valiant effort to right the apple cart, my own attorneys posed Munchy this single question: "Well, Rudy, how did you get the idea to write *The Shell Game* screenplay? How and when did you do it?"

Munchy answered them in true Munchy fashion. "Well, first," he said, "I poured myself a little tequila…. Then I squeezed a little lime in it…. Then I let the tequila mix with the lime…. And then I took a few sips and I let my mind wander, and I sat down at the computer, and it just came flowing out…."

I guess he figured if it worked once, why wouldn't it work again? Thankfully, my attorneys weren't quite as gullible as the adjunct Pepperdine professor and Munchy's testimony was quickly dismissed as the (costly and time consuming) meaningless ramblings of a lunatic.

CHAPTER 12

THE RUSH

MUNCHY'S RIDICULOUS, SELF-SERVING DEPOSITION was an unfortunate encounter with the surreal and did nothing to help me regain my faith in humanity. In fact, it had the opposite effect. This was someone with whom I had shared many years of time and experience, someone who claimed to be my friend. It's a sad fact that people as a species, even the ones closest to you, will often let you down. I hate to sound pessimistic, and I wish it wasn't true, but we can't ignore the reality of this fact any more than we can ignore the reality that, as disturbing and unlikely as it may have sounded at first, the Catholic church has long been running the world's largest ring of conspiratorial child molesters. The truth ain't always pretty, but that doesn't make it any less true.

When it came time for me to give my own deposition, things got a little crazy as well. Opposing counsel was not exactly what you'd describe as "friendly," and there was a bit of contention. There was also a very odd occurrence.

When there's a court case like this, the lawyers all do their diligent research, and through that research, they summon up all of the relevant witnesses they can find who are pertinent to the case. Once they have their list of witnesses, they call them all in to give their depositions. A deposition is just a fancy word for a recorded interview like you see on TV, where the witness is asked a bunch of questions and is supposed to tell everything they know about the matter at hand under oath. As a primary party, I was, of course, asked to give my own deposition. This was standard procedure. However, when it came time for me to get grilled, things got a little crazy.

Lead opposing counsel, who was a heavyset, pasty white, jowly, Jabba-the-Hutt-looking, smarmy, humorless man in his forties or fifties, began my interview in a highly accusatory fashion. His strategy seemed to be to try to turn the tables and make me out to be the bad guy. Can you imagine? This wasn't Nam; there were rules. Supposedly. Still, it didn't stop him.

"So, Mister Grosso, why should we believe you?" he started out. "What evidence do you have? You never met with Miramax, no one over there has ever heard of you, and you never spoke to anyone from Miramax or any of the writers or producers of *Rounders*. How do we know you didn't just make all this up? What evidence do you have that your ideas were used?"

"You mean besides the movie?" I retorted.

He didn't like that reply very much. He seemed a little taken aback and instantly became defensive.

"Well, uh, um, yes, we can agree that there are similarities. We'll get to those later, uh, but you're the one who wrote a book called *The Honest Con*, not my clients. How do we know you're not running some sort of con game right now?"

This insidious act of legal desperation was beyond absurd, even for a cornered, slimy lawyer, and I was truly shocked at the out-of-left-field, totally irrelevant nature of it. If I've learned anything in life, and I don't claim to have learned much, but if I've learned anything at all, it's that no brand of human can surprise you with just how scuzzy humans can be like a slimeball lawyer.

During the discovery phase of the case, I was instructed by Marder to provide samples of my writing. He wanted copies of everything I had ever done in order to prove I was actually a writer, or aspiring to be one, and not some crackpot who had never even scratched out a few lines on a cocktail napkin.

I followed orders and did as I was told. I submitted a whole pile of stuff I had worked on over the years—everything from partial screenplays to short stories, to feature articles, to *Poker Digest* columns, to poems and song lyrics. One of the pieces, among the dozens I had turned in, was a short story I had written called "The Honest Con," and Jabba decided to use this particular title to take an idiotic dig at me, stating that since I had written a story called

"The Honest Con," I must be some sort of con man. His theory was unfounded, baseless, ludicrous, and laughable.

"What are you talking about?" was my reply. "First of all, it's not a book, it's a short story, and it doesn't have anything to do with poker or movies or me conning anyone. It's about a woman in Montana."

"Uh-huh," he snorted, like he had made his point and scored one for his team. But I guess even Jabba figured he'd milked that fantasy cow long enough because he quickly dropped the subject and returned to his original tack. That's when the incident occurred.

"So you admit you had no interaction with anyone from Miramax at any time, nor did you have any interaction with any of the writers or producers of *Rounders*. You never had a single meeting with any of them or even a phone call."

"That's correct."

"Well then," he said arrogantly. He sat down and relaxed a bit now, like his work was just about done. "How could they have possibly stolen your ideas?"

"I sent my script to a company called Gotham Entertainment Group that was located in the same building as Miramax at 99 Hudson Street in New York. Gotham was started by Miramax employees and had a first-look deal…"

Right then, I was interrupted by a commotion. As soon as the words "Gotham Entertainment Group" escaped my lips, a casually dressed Miramax representative, who had been sitting silently throughout the proceedings looking rather bored up until then, suddenly broke out of his stupor. He was short, dressed in jeans and a rugby shirt, and had a thick black Magnum, P.I. mustache and a full head of bushy black hair that made him look like a throwback to the seventies. He sure was agile, though, this I can guarantee, and faster than he looked. The second I mentioned Gotham, his eyes got really big, the mustache twitched noticeably, he bolted upright, and without saying a word, jumped out of his chair and ran clear out of the room. I mean literally ran, like as fast as he could go. He crashed through the doors and was gone in about two seconds, never to return. It was quite bizarre, but it seemed pretty obvious I'd touched a nerve.

He must have been under orders to sit in on the proceedings and report back to his bosses in New York as to whether or not I had a case. My guess is that once he heard me mention Gotham, he must have told them, "Yes," despite my having been rudely and inappropriately mislabeled a "con man" simply because I had written a story with that word in the title. People are funny. No doubt about it.

CHAPTER 13

THE TURN

WHEN MAGNUM JR. AND HIS anachronistic stache scampered out of that deposition room like a scared rabbit, it seemed obvious that people were paying attention to this thing. I was right, and I knew it. And when I saw that little bit of odd drama unfold, I really knew it. As did they. But that was still very early on in the proceedings before any of the rulings had come down. We were way past that now.

Despite the court initially dismissing the case for a "lack of substantial similarity between the two works"—the most absurd and wrong decision ever made by a court of law— thanks to Marder and his "breach of implied contract" gambit and subsequent victory in the appeals court, we had a breath of new life. We were still in the game, and we had momentum on our side. Following the appeals court win, the case had made major news. Marder was famous. The goddamned California Lawyer of the Year. The internets were ablaze. Bigshots were worried, wringing their hands, pulling their hair plugs out. We had the similarities, despite what that stupid first judge said. We had the access theory. Solid. And now we had this implied contract angle. Things were looking up. I can't say I was out shopping for yachts, but I was fairly confident that my troubles would soon be over.

We had changed the law. My name was now inscribed in all the law books. Ole Sasqy, setting precedent. Can you believe it? They actually started to teach classes on my case in college—and not just in law schools but business schools as well. It's true. I was now the unwitting subject of college classes rather than the long-haired, barefoot rebel student. Crazy how things work out. It was a big deal. We had done it. Victory was at hand. All we needed to do now was run it up the flagpole again and let logic and reason rule the day. And that's what we did.

After we won the appeal, we resubmitted the case to state court, and we waited. There was a lot of waiting. Years and years of waiting.

And it was then, after yet another excruciating, many-years-long waiting period that the case took another unfathomable turn.

The Los Angeles Municipal Court judge who was tasked with making the final ruling, the one that would make or break us for good after nearly ten years of struggle and strife the likes of which my stoic Sicilian great-grandparents had never even seen, dismissed the case. The mother-loving judge dismissed the case. Again. And here's the kicker. He acknowledged that there were substantial similarities.

Finally. He basically said that given the similarities of the two works and the timing in which they were created, "an inference may be made that some of the ideas expressed in both works may have had a common host."

The two works may have had a "common host," meaning that one could believe that both stemmed from the same place. Since I had written mine first, I believed I was the host. This sounded to me like an offhanded way of saying that they were guilty as sin, that they had used my script to make theirs. To me, it was clear as crystal. But somehow, it didn't matter. And why not? Here's the bigger kicker—the kicker to end all kickers.

Unbelievably, astonishingly, the judge dismissed the case on the grounds that "Grosso failed to establish any connection between Gotham Entertainment Group and Miramax." (See Extra Bullet Two.)

That was his ruling. To this day, it mystifies me to no end. It is awfully hard to believe and even harder to swallow. He might as well have dismissed the case on the grounds that "Grosso is a known alien from the planet Quazark and therefore has no rights as an Earthling." I was utterly dumbfounded and distraught.

Not only had I established a connection between the two companies, but the connection that I established couldn't be any more obvious and overt. I had all the evidence in the world to support my claim. It's all a matter of public record. It's not some deep and unspoken secret I had to dig up from a dark and well-concealed hiding place. There are multiple news stories about it all over the web.

It is even detailed in the aptly titled book *Down and Dirty Pictures: Miramax, Sundance, and the Rise of Independent Film*. In it, the author, Peter Biskind, discusses all the parties involved, including firsthand descriptions of Miramax in the early days. It talks about how aggressively dishonest they were and how they would rather screw you over than work with you on the level, even if the deal was already in their favor. At one point in the book, a producer who worked directly with Harvey Weinstein describes him as "a push-cart peddler who is more than happy to put his thumb on the scale when the old lady is buying meat." It also mentions Gotham Entertainment Group executive Patrick McDarrah by name and shows him lounging on the Miramax yacht in Cannes in 1994, just two years before I sent him my script at Gotham. It was the easiest research I ever did. But this judge, the honorable Los Angeles Superior Court Judge Edward Ferns, in his infinite wisdom, somehow couldn't see it. Or maybe he chose not to.

It's like the further down the rabbit hole I went, the weirder it got. Black was white. Up was down. Wrong was right. And no one seemed to care. The truth was just an undefined, ethereal fantasy that had no place in reality and no chance of ever congealing into anything that could be touched or felt. It had no impact. You couldn't pick it up. You couldn't throw it. It took up no space, held no weight, and could only be seen by those special few who were immediately deemed crazy outsiders by those in power. Crazy outsiders, the kind the entrenched elite didn't even want skulking around their town, let alone swimming in their pool. Truth and its fraternal twin, Justice, only existed as vague Promethean concepts in some other faraway and unknown realm—one that owned no real estate in the dreamless, grease-stained, asphalt wasteland of modern Los Angeles.

It was as if the judge had just stated that the world was actually flat and one plus one equals thirty-seven, and that was the end of it. And so we lost. Somehow. Or rather, I lost. Marder did just fine. Shortly after that last, insane final decision, he vacated his high-rise octagonal office and started his own practice focusing solely on copyright infringement cases. Why not? He had the juice. He changed the law. He was famous. He was now known as the go-to guy in town if your ideas had been stolen. He did very well for himself. As a matter of fact, for the first six months or so he was in business under his own banner, he would regularly call me on the phone to inform me of his latest victories.

"Jeff," he would say, "you won't believe it. I just got three million for this guy and five million for so and so and six million for this one…." He would go on to tell me how they all owed me a huge debt of gratitude, how without me, they would never have had a case to pursue, yada, yada.

"Great," I would respond, "tell them all I'll happily accept ten percent from each." Needless to say, I never got 10 percent or any percent. Not even a goddamned fruit basket. Eventually, Marder stopped calling.

That final decision was a tough moment for me, to be sure. It was extremely difficult to acknowledge that it was all over, that I would have no further recourse. They had simply gotten away with it, and that was all there was to it. The bad guys had spent over three million dollars in reported legal costs, and they had won. It wasn't easy to face defeat after so many years. Especially in such an absurd and outrageous fashion.

The exchange I had with Marder immediately following that final decision was one I will never forget. I remember him vividly, leaning back in his chair after I had asked him what in holy hell had just happened and him coolly answering, "Jeff, all I can tell you is that some of these guys play golf together."

"Some of these guys play golf together" was a lawyer's way of saying the system was corrupt.

Marder's breach of implied contract appeal was successful enough for him to extend the case just long enough for him to achieve his own fame and glory by changing the law but not quite far enough for us to actually win the case. Marder may have been a golfer himself. I don't know. All I know is that I am not a golfer. I prefer tennis. It's a lot harder to cheat.

CHAPTER 14

THE CATCH

THE FIRST TEXAS HOLD'EM POKER tournament I ever participated in was a sixty-dollar buy-in tournament that they ran daily at the Hollywood Park Casino in Inglewood, CA. Tournaments are fun, as you can't lose any more than the cost of the buy-in, and you have the potential to win a good amount of money. First place prize money for the tournament that day was one thousand dollars. Plus, they take up a lot of time—several hours or more—so you are able to play a ton of hands for just a nominal entry fee, which is good practice. I still enjoy playing in the occasional tournament.

Hollywood Park was a famous horse-racing track that had a casino attached to it on the same grounds. They staged this particular tournament every day at 11 a.m., and it usually drew a fair crowd of players despite the hour. This first one that I was playing in started out with about forty entrants. After a few hours of playing, much to my delight, as it was my inaugural turn, we were down to just five play-ers, of which I was one.

The tournament that day, for some inexplicable rea-son, had drawn quite a substantial and raucous crowd of onlookers. They were much more numerous and much louder than your regular crowd of looky-loos and hang-ers-on that I had seen bird-dogging these tournaments on prior occasions. I don't know if it was two-for-one kamika-zes in the bar that day or what, but the air was charged with the energy of a long-awaited prize fight. The atmosphere was drenched in a palpable hostility, which manifested itself mainly in the colorful contingent who had carved out turf for themselves directly behind where I was seated. They were surly, unruly, and pacing around in a tight circle like a platoon of POWs scanning the hurricane-fenced perimeter of the prison camp, anxiously awaiting an opportunity to break through. One of their buddies was evidently still alive in the tournament with me, and judging from their "human powder kegs looking for a spark" demeanor, some or all of them must have owned a portion of his hide.

As is commonplace in card rooms and casinos all over the world, it appeared that this gentleman, who was skillful and/or lucky enough to still be alive in this tournament, most likely didn't have the sixty-dollar entry fee he needed to initially buy in. Therefore, to gain entrance into the tour-nament, he had no doubt received "backing" by a friend or friends in exchange for a percentage of his winnings should he indeed make it far enough to "cash." Backing players is a well-known and common practice on all levels, small and large, as the capricious nature of the game often makes it difficult for even the best players to remain consistently flush. Bankrolls come and go like Amazon Prime delivery people. They're here, and then they're gone.

Sometimes a highly skilled player will just have gone bust, but he will still, of course, want to remain in action. This is where the backers come in. It seemed likely that someone had given this particular doodle the sixty-dollar buy-in in exchange for receiving half of his winnings should he be able to cash, meaning he finishes in first, second, or third place, or whichever place that particular tournament paid down to. Perhaps two backers each put in thirty dollars and agreed to split their share of the winnings or three put in twenty dollars each. There was no way of knowing the specific details, but it was obvious some such bargain had been struck, as this group of supporters was bombastically rooting, hooting, hollering, kibitzing, and generally just loudly carrying on like a pack of wild banshees at a malt liquor convention.

"He ain't got nothing! Raise him! Raise him!" they would scream, even if they had not seen their boy's cards and had no factual knowledge of his opponent's hand. They seemed almost omniscient in their understanding of how he should play, although they were almost invariably wrong. Doodle had succeeded thus far mainly by ignoring them, and smartly.

"Why'd you call that? What are you, stupid?" they would vehemently wonder out loud after he had proven to be beaten at the end of a hand. "You knew he had the flush!"It went on and on like that all morning. They either had a vested interest in this player or were just drunk and crazy. Or possibly some combination thereof. At one point, the hell-raising boiled over to such an extent that the meek and mild tournament director was forced to construct a makeshift barrier of chairs to prevent the mob from over-running the table.

We played for a while longer under the ominous gaze of the crowd. I made some moves, caught some cards, and sent a few players packing. Suddenly, there were just two of us left. It was down to me and doodle, with the insane clown posse fan base, which was now more out of control than ever. How the tournament director allowed this scene to unfold or even why it was unfolding—all over this silly little daily tournament—remains a mystery to me to this day. Some things just can't be explained.

So now doodle and I are "heads-up," one on one, mano y mano, and the onlookers are basically part of the action. They take turns actually sitting down at the table next to their guy until the dealer informs them that this is not allowed. They're all playing along with him and against me. We each have about an equal amount of chips, and I'm ready for this thing to be over. I want to win and split. I've had enough, and I'm feeling kind of anxious and threatened. It was like playing poker in the Thunderdome. But now, with only two of us left, I surmised that the end should come fairly quickly. It couldn't come quick enough for me. As we were about to start the first heads-up hand, the crowd was gaining manic momentum and haranguing me to no end.

"You got him! You got him! He got no game! You got him! Take him down!" they yelled. I didn't even look back over my shoulder. I pretended to be oblivious. I can feel hot alcoholic breath on the back of my neck, and it's more than a little unnerving. Under extreme pressure, the dealer shuffled and dealt out the cards. This was the first hand with just the two of us left, and I received the ace and seven of hearts. Now this is not a great starting Hold'em hand when playing against a full table of nine players—fair to middling maybe—but heads-up, one on one, it's pretty darn good. Good enough for me at that point anyway. The zoo-like conditions were a bit much. It was my first goddamned tournament, and I wasn't accustomed to the heated air of violence. At least not on this level. I wanted to win and I wanted out of there in just about equal amounts. With very little hesitation, I decided to make my big play with this hand. It was time to decide this thing one way or the other.

Now as you may or may not already know, there are two distinct versions of Texas Hold'em: limit and no-limit. The games are played the same way with the same rules, but the betting structures are different. In Limit Hold'em, the betting is confined to whatever limit you are playing. If you are playing three to six dollars, all the bets are made in increments of three or six dollars. You can raise, of course, but if you raise a six-dollar bet, you can only raise it exactly six dollars. No more and no less. In no-limit however, bets are made in any amount you like. If you have $500 in chips on the table and you want to bet it all at once, you can. If you wish to bet exactly $134 or just one dollar or anything in between, you can do that as well. And you can do this at any time there is a betting round.

The tournament I was currently mired in, unlike the regular live-action Limit Hold'em I normally played, was no-limit. There were no incremental limits to constrain your betting. If you felt like shoving all your chips in at once, you were allowed to do so at any given time. No-limit Hold'em is the game that is normally shown on TV and in the movies, such as *Rounders*, as removing the limits makes for more dramatic action. I was currently ready to take some action of my own.

"I'm all in," I said as I pushed all of my chips into the middle of the table. This move prompted an unrestrained uproar from the miscreant support group. They took turns dive bombing the table, looking at their guy's cards, which he showed them all freely, and screaming at each other, arguing fervently over what he should do.

"Call him! Call him! Kid ain't got nothing! He bluffing! He bluffing!" one supporter hollered. This would be met with a vociferous rebuttal from a supporter with a differing opinion. "Dump it! Dump it! Wait for a better hand! Don't go down with that garbage!"

In the end, Team Call was evidently louder and more convincing than Team Fold, and they eventually drowned out the other side. Abiding the mad consensus of his clan, doodle shoved all of his chips into the center of the table and called me. He had a few more chips than I did, so if he won this hand, he would win the tournament and take home first place and one thousand dollars in prize money. I would receive the second-place prize of $550, which is way better than nothing but a bit like kissing your sister, especially after all I'd been through.

At this point, we were both all in, so no more betting could occur. The outcome of this hand would decide the winner of the tourney. There was no turning back now. It would all be over in a matter of moments. It was in God's hands now. As was customary when this situation arose, with no more bets to be made, we each exposed our cards. Doodle turned over two threes. Pocket threes. He had a pair. A small pair, but a pair. Not bad. He had a pair, and I had no pair, which meant that I would have to match either my ace or my seven on the board—or catch three or more hearts to make a flush—in order to beat him. So far, he was ahead of me with his threes. But there were more cards to come.

Amidst the deafening cacophony of the crowd, the dealer spread the flop. Miraculously, for me, it came the ace of diamonds, the seven of spades, and the two of clubs. This was a dream flop for me. I now had two pair, aces and sevens, against his puny pair of threes. I remained silent, but I was internally elated, while the railbirds lost their minds. They started calling me names of all kinds in a variety of broken languages and hurling such hatred in my direction that one would think I had just occupied France.

"Son-of-a-bitch! Motherfucker! Kid got lucky! Lucky fucker! Is the dealer your brother?!" And so on and so forth. They were in a suicidal tizzy. The groans emitting from them sounded like the groans one would make upon learning your favorite dog had just died or a tree had just fallen on your house. Looking increasingly more and more frightened, the dealer nervously dealt out the turn card. It was the ten of clubs. This card was no help to either of us, but more importantly, it was of no help to him. I was already way in the lead with my "aces up" and happy as a clam.

Another loud moan erupted from the backers. They were slapping their heads and gripping the brass railing that bordered the poker room like they wanted to rip it out of the floor. I had never seen such maniacal emotion expressed over such a little podunk card game in my life. I had no idea what was going on, but I had to just deal with it. I had no other choice.

There was just one more card to come. It was all but over. I was about to be crowned champion of the day, much to the dismay of the angry and charged-up peanut gallery. And let's face it, these were bad peanuts. There's no way they would pass inspection as the Planter's factory. That guy with the top hat and the cane would boot them right out the door.

At this point in the action, my opponent actually stood up, as he prepared to embark on his walk of shame toward the second-place prize money followed soon after by the exit (or more likely the bar), as he knew in his heart that his measly little threes were soundly and roundly beaten by my mighty and noble aces and sevens. The only thing that could possibly save him at this point would be if another three somehow fell on the river. He already had two threes in his hand, which left just two threes unaccounted for. With just over forty cards left in the deck, this made his odds of catching that third three 20-1 or worse. I was not worried in the slightest. I was a lock. I was sitting in the catbird seat and already planning on how to spend the first-place prize loot. Hookers and blow, obviously.

The crowd was now reminiscent of the crowd one would find at the Roman Colosseum during a slave battle to the death. They were openly bloodthirsty and out of control. The dealer was sweating profusely, wiping his brow repeatedly with a handkerchief. The tournament director had bailed. He was nowhere to be seen. He had vacated the scene entirely, the coward. With hands that were shaking noticeably, the dealer somehow managed to peel off the fifth and final card amidst the mean and anxious roar of the crowd.

The three of spades fell on the river like an extinction-level event, the sum total of every nightmare I'd ever had. I literally couldn't believe my eyes. The audience exploded. They started doing backflips and cartwheels all down the gaudy, dirty carpet of the card room floor. It was like a mangy, drunken circus had come to town. They acted like they had all just won the billion-dollar Powerball jackpot. I was crushed. At that moment, I knew exactly what a field goal kicker feels like when he shanks the game-winner off of the goal post with no time left in a championship game. *Pain*. Tremendous amounts of pain.

What went wrong? How could I lose? How did this happen?

Easy. 20-1 is not 100-1 or 1000-1; it's just 20-1. It's far from impossible and not too far from almost likely. Not likely maybe but not extremely unlikely. It's just 20-1, and it happens all the time. Every hour of every day. "That's poker," as they say. Indeed, it is. And that's what makes it so alluring. Anything can happen at any time, and it usually does.

It's that card. It's that 20-1 shot, thousand-dollar card that falls like a flaming meteor onto the soft green surface of your world and either brings forth genesis for a new and wonderful life in the garden or completely wipes out your civilization. But whether it thrills or kills, it's one flashing moment of rocket-fueled, lightning-pumping, fire-breathing fury. And that, my friend, is why we play the game.

CHAPTER 15

THE RIVER

THIS MIGHT SOUND HARD TO believe, but I really don't gamble very much or very often, and even when I do, it's always for paltry stakes.

"But you play poker," you might say. Yes, this is true, but poker is not gambling. Why? Because you don't play against the house. You play against other people. The house just takes a rake of every pot. This rake alone can make it very difficult to beat some games, especially at the lower limits, true, but my point is that with poker, you aren't trying to beat the house. You are just trying to best the other players at the table. Attempting to beat the house is a sucker's bet. The house always wins. Always. They don't build multi-billion-dollar casinos because the odds aren't in their favor.

Somewhere in the middle of my ten-year slog of a court case, the Disney corporation bought Miramax Film Co. I don't know precisely why the deal was made, but it sure wouldn't surprise me if the plethora of lawsuits that were pending against Miramax, mine being one of them, had something to do with it. Not to mention what must have seemed like an endless parade of sexual assault and harassment allegations that had been levied against ole Harvey Weinstein. Allegations and their accompanying lawsuits that must have had him mired up to his neck on a daily basis.

The sale of the company to Disney had a drastic impact on my case, at least in my personal opinion. Suddenly, I was no longer suing Miramax, which was a New York-based company well-known for shady dealings, helmed by individuals everyone loathed. I was now suing Disney, a gigantic, Los Angeles-based corporation that pretty much owned the state of California, if not the world, and was helmed by Mickey Mouse. Suddenly, the "house" I was taking on was one of the most powerful corporations on the planet with tentacles that reached, like the Ursula character in *The Little Mermaid*, into every aspect of Southern California life and well beyond. The mouse was huge. The mouse was global. The mouse carried a ton of weight. The mouse drew a lot of water in this town. I didn't draw shit.

And yes, I was absolutely much more comfortable fighting Miramax, against whom I felt we really had a decent chance of winning, especially after Marder changed the law. It looked like things were finally going our way. We had built up some momentum, and we had the truth on our side. But now we were taking on the mouse, which was a very enormous, powerful, and ferocious animal to slay. Too enormous. Too powerful. And too ferocious. And I knew it.

I knew as soon as it happened that we were now going to be embroiled in a whole other level of warfare.

The day I was informed of Miramax's sale to Disney, both my stomach and my hopes sank like a rock in a fish tank. Sadly, it turns out that I was right. As you have now seen for yourself in the form of the ludicrous final decision rendered by the judge in this case, the one that vanquished it for good, the fix was in. The mouse had rigged the game. I never had a chance.

"Trust everyone, but always cut the cards." Indeed. Words to live by.

CHAPTER 16

THE CAKE

BY THE TIME OF MY college graduation, the idea of writing a poker movie specifically about Texas Hold'em—one that was based on my own experiences in the card clubs—had, of course, already occurred to me. The first thing they teach you in school is "Write what you know." And that was what I knew. It was pretty much *all* I knew, at least thus far. But I wasn't ready to strap myself down and commit to writing a screenplay just yet. I had just wrapped-up nearly twenty years of straight schooling. I needed a break.

What I really longed for was some exposure to something new and exotic. Something I knew nothing about. I was anxious to be immersed in whatever remote and unknown counter-sub-culture I could find. I had grown up reading Hunter S. Thompson and Tom Wolfe, and I was ready to start experiencing some real-life adventures beyond Malibu and Gardena. I wanted to broaden my horizons. I had a naturally inquisitive nature, and I was always itching to learn new things—especially the stuff they didn't teach you in school. Despite my unique and colorful experiences in the world of poker and card clubs, that was just one subculture of many. I knew how naive and inexperienced I was, and I didn't like it.

Right along these lines, I had a full-blown lunatic of an uncle who lived off the grid down in the Florida Keys. He was commonly known as *Tricky* or *Trick* for reasons that became all too apparent as soon as you met him. Tricky, in a word, was *tricky*.

Despite the trickiness, daily danger, and generally irresponsible nature of it, one could argue that my Key West trip with Tricky was, on some level at least, educational. I wanted adventure, and it delivered. I craved exposure to interesting characters and culture, and I got that as well. In spades. I was young and naïve, and I wanted to learn. And learn I did. It turned out to be everything Tricky said it was and much more.

The experience truly changed my life forever and still resonates soundly with me to this day. Many years after that trip and well after all of the *Shell Game / Rounders* brouhaha had come and gone, I ended up writing a book about my time there called *Key Waste: Swinging with Savages in the Conch Republic*. I later turned that book into a screenplay titled *Greetings from Key West*, which actually at one point attracted some interest from a semi-legitimate Hollywood producer. I kid you not. I wasn't going to let the whole *Rounders* disaster put me off my dream forever. As difficult as it was to accept that I had been robbed, cheated, and damned, what was I supposed to do? I wasn't dead. I had to move on and try something else. I had no other choice, and I was nothing if not intrepid.

Well, after having adapted my Key West book into a feature screenplay, by sheer blind luck I happened upon a decent Hollywood connection through the cousin of my friend Barney whom I had known since college and who would later become my ersatz "manager." Through this cousin connection, whose name was Vinny, a fellow Italian paisan from New Jersey, we were able to actually get the Key West script into the hands of a credited producer, who actually read it and liked it. Crazy, I know. But true. I had his nose open. People were getting involved. Wheels were turning. Machinations were mechanizing. There was a buzz in the air. It looked like the good guys might actually win one for a change. This fucking guy wanted to make the movie. God bless him. And we wanted him to make it. We were all on the same page. Terms were negotiated and agreed upon. Contracts were drafted. Parties were excited. It was a heady time.

However, after receiving many pages of notes and executing several rewrites and after two different sets of contracts were drawn and presented to me on two different occasions—for reasons that are still to this day unclear—Mr. Producer Man walked away from the project at the eleventh hour, never to return. Poof. Vanished into thin air. Zero explanation. Gone with the wind. Why? Who knows? He just walked away after all that. It was unbelievable. I won't kid you. That one hurt a lot. We were seemingly so close, and I had worked so hard to no avail. Again.

So what happened then? Did I give up? Did I discard my dream and bury my head in the sand, too discouraged and depressed to continue?

Oh, hell no. My ever-loving mother didn't raise me to go knock-kneed at the first sign of adversity. Or even the second sign. Or the third. I licked my wounds, which were deep, and went back to the drawing board.

As luck would have it, Barney, sometimes known as *Admiral Barney* for reasons that would only become clear to you if you read yet another one of my unproduced screenplays, took our vanishing producer predicament to heart. God bless him. After a month or so had passed since Mr. Producer Man ghosted the *Greetings from Key West* movie project, Barney actually managed to score us a semi-legitimate Hollywood meeting with a woman named Karen Strongman, only she preferred to go by Karen *Strongwoman*, which should tell you a lot about her right there.

Barney had met her through some other relative, a great aunt from Des Moines or something who had gone to college with her a million years ago—thank God for Barney's extended family—and she actually agreed to meet with us, which was amazing enough in its own right. She claimed to have some decent connections around town, including one connection to, amazingly enough, Steven freaking Spielberg.

This was quite a coup for a couple of scrubbies like us, and we were taking it seriously. It was to be a breakfast meeting, and Strongwoman was gracious enough to host it at her own home, which was located high in the Hollywood Hills. Barney had gone all out for the occasion and baked one of his famous Italian ricotta cheesecakes. Yes, my manager bakes. Thank goodness. We weren't going to be arriving empty handed. Not us. Mom would be proud. We were chock full of homemade goodness and grit, as was the cake.

We hopped in my van and headed out, freeway bound and headstrong. After a little traffic congestion and a few wrong turns, we eventually managed to locate the right address, which happened to be a stalwart house way up on a steep hillside. There was a long, very steep driveway leading up to a garage somewhere out of sight and a gate at the bottom that was open, yet didn't seem appropriate for us to pass through, particularly not on our first visit. Hence, we parked on the street and faced the mountainous staircase that led up to the front door like two hapless, alpine adventurers who had lost their way in the Andes.

"Jesus, did you bring oxygen, Barney?" I quipped, gearing up for the climb.

"Nope, just cheesecake," he replied squarely. "You're on your own."

Standard. As we climbed the thousand stairs up to her house—Barney dutifully toting the heavy glass dish of Italian ricotta cheesecake—I quietly tittered at the notion that she could possibly really know ole Stevey. I was planning a strategy where I could politely inquire along those lines, but of course, there was no need. Like all of them, with no provocation whatsoever, she name-dropped like a B-2 bomber over Baghdad.

It turned out that not only did she indeed know him, but they were close friends. Allegedly. According to her. But still, friends with Spielberg...not too shabby. And here I am suddenly, in her house drinking French press coffee with foam, picking politely from a tray of fresh raspberries, eating Barney's Italian ricotta cheesecake. I actually almost felt like I was in Hollywood for a moment.

I feel like I should mention that there was very weird artwork hung all over the house, including a child-like, semi-impressionistic painting of Elvis naked, standing in the middle of the desert next to a cactus. Not only was the King sporting full frontal nudity, but this was the painting that greeted us right as we walked in the front door at the top of the stairs, a thousand feet above the street below. This bizarre Elvis painting had been given the most exclusive and important wall-space real estate. You couldn't miss it. It was the first thing you saw when you entered the domicile.

"Was that naked Elvis I passed on the way in?" I asked innocently, just to make conversation as we entered the strange, hilltop chalet and said our hellos.

"Yes. That's our naked Elvis to greet you right at the top of the stairs."

"Great, I love Elvis. I'm more used to him with clothes on, but still...."

In addition to allegedly knowing Spielberg and possessing a painting of Elvis naked, this special lady also had a bona-fide Hollywood pedigree.

Her father was a very well-known, Academy Award-winning director who had won not one but three Oscars. I kid you not. That part of the narrative was true and proven, which also lent credence to her Spielberg rap and made our being there all that much more rare and unusual.

Barney and I had already laid some groundwork before this highly anticipated meeting, so I was feeling confident and truly believed this may actually lead to something real. But even so, reaching this point didn't come without its challenges.

For starters, when Barney first emailed her and mentioned our predicament with my unproduced screenplay and vanishing producer, her snap response was, "Tell him to enter a screenwriting contest."

Standard blowoff. We were made of tougher stock than that. We weren't going to give up that easy. We emailed her back and attempted to convey that we were really past the contest stage. We informed her that we'd already had some interest, had almost gotten it made with a legitimate producer, etc. to which she would say, "Okay, I will read it, but can I do it later? I'm busy. I have a new script of my own I'm working on, my producer is waiting for it, my cat is sick, I have a broken toe..." etc.

Standard blowoff number two. To which we replied, persistent as a car salesman, "No, I'm sorry. We really can't wait. Just please read the first five pages, and if it doesn't hook you, just delete and forget about it."

I figured it would only take her a few minutes to read five pages. If she wasn't thrilled, she could just blow the whole thing off and we'd chalk it up to experience. But I also knew that the first five pages set a pretty nice hook. Well, unsurprisingly, many weeks went by without a word.

I honestly didn't expect much. I figured my communication style was too aggressive, and it was a zillion-to-one shot she would ever even open the screenplay file. But lo and behold, one day she up and replied.

"I read your friend's script! I thought it was charming, well written, and commercial."

That's what we call in the biz the Rush review, as in the band Rush, who are known by their fans as *The Holy Triumvirate*. This was the holy triumvirate of high praise from about as high a source as you could ever hope to find. At least for nobody scruffians like us. That's the good news. The bad news is, she went on to say, "I don't know what you hope to gain from me reading it, but I'd be happy to discuss it."

This seemed ludicrous on its face. How could she not know what we hoped to gain? We hoped to gain her helping us get it to someone who could help us make it, of course, which was spelled out perfectly in clean English in the email. We had clearly stated that we were interested in her helping us get it into the hands of a producer, or production company, or studio, or Spielberg, or what have you. That was the stated goal. It wasn't a mystery. And, of course, she would be compensated and credited for her involvement should anything come to fruition. Astonishingly, she seemed to either not understand this obvious concept or was playing dumb for some unknown reason. But at least she was willing to discuss it, which was something.

So, us being us, we played along—we didn't have anything better to do—and asked her to meet us for lunch, but she was, of course, much too busy for that. She did, however, happen to by chance have from 9:00 a.m. to 10:30 a.m. free on such and such a date, and if we liked, we could just come to her house to make it all the more convenient.

Well, we took the bait and bit down hard. Why not? We gussied up the best we could and went to the meeting at her fancy-pants house in the hills. We climbed the thousand stairs and took our assigned places at the table with the elegant dishes and the French coffee and the foam and the raspberries and the cheesecake Barney brought—with naked Elvis presiding over the whole thing—and all of us crunched into this little breakfast nook by the window even though the house was huge, and she proceeded to beat the ever-living crap out of me for eighty-five minutes.

When we got back in the van afterwards, the first thing Barney said to me was, "Whipple, do you need a steak for your eye?" He called me Whipple after a character in one of my screenplays. And he was right. I did need a steak. She beat me like eggs that need to go into a quiche. She beat me like Mike Tyson in his prime. She beat me like it was her job and it was work she enjoyed.

"You're not special," was her favorite line. She used that one about ten times, even though we'd just met.

"You're not special," she said matter-of-factly, eyes cold as cast iron left outdoors in a Cleveland winter.

"I'm not?"

"No."

"Not even a little?"

"No."

Straight-faced. No smile. Not even a smirk.

Then she told me that in order to solve my dilemma, I should write letters to the agents of people I wanted to work with in Hollywood. She said that I should "go on IMDB, get the names of agents, and write them letters."

Write blind letters to agents. This was her big advice.

Obsequious and respectful as I was trying to be, and as in awe and enamored of the company and surroundings as I truly was, I could only remain on my best behavior for so long. The "write letters to agents" rap, like a sharp and swift arrow launched from a fully extended 100-pound compound bow, instantly penetrated the thin veneer of my manners and lodged itself right in the heart of my angry Sasquatch nerve center.

I had tried to remain civil and professional. She had agreed to meet with us, and I appreciated that immensely. She was certainly under no obligation to do so. But after being told I wasn't special a few dozen times and that my salvation lied in writing cold-call letters to fucking Hollywood agents, well, at that point, I got hot. The war was on, and the gloves were off. But of course, I never had a chance. I was out-manned, or more precisely, *out-womaned*. It was like the last round of the fight at the end of *Rocky*. Actually, it was more like the first fight in *Rocky III*, and she was Clubber Lang. At one point, I threatened to go outside and blow my brains out on her front lawn.

"You have to be willing to die for it," she said.

"Oh, I'm willing to die for it. I'm going to go outside right now and blow my brains out in your front yard. I have a loaded forty-five in my glove box. It won't be pretty, but the good news is, you guys can serve the leftover cheesecake at the wake. It won't even be stale. The funeral will be tomorrow."

Then she called me "angry" and said I had the wrong attitude while she snatched her laptop off the counter, opened it, and prepared to read me a letter she once sent to Paul Newman. This letter had allegedly convinced him to act in a movie that she had written and directed herself—the only one she had ever been able to get made, even with her connections. But still, not bad. She had gotten one made, which is way more than most of us, and with Paul stinking Newman as the lead. But before she started reading the letter, she buttered up the intro first.

"Now this is a very special letter," she said, her tone quiet and serious like she was in church and God himself was hanging on every word. "It's actually more of a poem. I worked on it for two weeks to get it just right. This isn't an ordinary letter. I don't expect you to be able to write a letter like this, but you can write your own from your own heart, and you can use this one for inspiration…."

Then she cleared her throat and paused until she had our full attention.

"Dear Paul…when my father, the director, took me to see *Butch Cassidy and the Sundance Kid* in the theater when I was in high school, I was blown away by how *real* you were…."

Needless to say, I'm all wound up by now and not willing to go gently into the naked Elvis Strongwoman goodnight of this morning cheesecake and raspberry psych ward meeting. Therefore, breaking every Hollywood moray and utterly violating the unspoken respect we are expected to have, as we knelt penitently at the feet of this all-knowing immaculate feminine oracle, I very rudely interrupted her in the middle of the first sentence of her recitation and blurted out, "Of course they would read your letter. Your father is famous and won three Oscars. But they're not going to read mine. It'll go right in the garbage." At which point, she glared at me like she was trying to turn me into a pillar of salt, angrily slammed the laptop closed, and threw it back on the counter behind her. Then she started back in with the body blows.

"You don't deserve to hear my letter," she scolded me. "You have the wrong attitude. You're not special," she reiterated as she rolled up a copy of *Variety* and proceeded to beat me over the head with it like a bad dog until it shredded in her hand. Metaphorically speaking.

She went on and on about how hard it is to make it in Hollywood and how much harder it is now than it used to be and how studios only make superhero movies now and how there's a million starving people in a small room all fighting over the same piece of stale bread and how Napoleon used to pick his generals for battle by asking them if they "felt lucky" that day, and I was like, "What? Why are we talking about Napoleon? This isn't a historical picture...."

I took it all in stride the best I could and responded, "I feel lucky as fuck, but it won't get my Judd Apatow love letter over the giant wall-pile of crap sent in by every other maggot in the world trying to do the same thing." And then she'd pummel me some more, after which I would feel bad that I had hurt her feelings, so I'd backpedal and apologize. I'd turn the love and praise shower back on and tell her how wonderful and brave she was, and eventually she'd pull out the laptop again and continue reading the magic letter....

"Paul...your integrity, your honesty, when you were in *The Hustler* and when you were in *Cool Hand Luke*...I BELIEVED you, and again in *The Color of Money*, your presence..."

And, of course, I'd lose it again, break in, and interrupt her.

"Do you really think if I write a love letter to Jeff Bridges or Woody Harrelson courtesy of CAA they're even going to get the letter, let alone open and read it?"

Slam! She'd close the laptop again and throw it back on the counter. This happened four or five times. All she wants to do is get through reading this fucking letter, and I just won't let her.

It was quite the scene, let me tell you. I'm still not sure if she ever actually got to the end of the damn thing or not. Hollywood is a very strange place. This fact is inarguable.

What does it all mean? The same thing it always means. Another promise broken. Another dream shattered like an empty sugar-glass beer bottle hurled against the hard, heartless exoskeleton of showbiz. Another opportunity turning out to have not been one at all, save another opportunity to endure further pain, humiliation, and rejection.

When you're young, they tell you to follow your dream. Listen to your heart, they say. Believe in your passion, whatever it may be. They shower you with platitudes like "Do what you love, and the success will follow." I suppose this is fairly sound advice. We're each born with just one ticket, good for only one ride, and they aren't giving out any more of them. They don't sell them, no matter how much money you have. It doesn't matter who you know or how important you may be. It's a one-and-done-type deal, and you never know how long the ride is going to last. Every one is different, so you may as well make the best of it. Follow your dream, they say....

But at what cost? And for how long? These are questions that they don't answer. Suppose you try your very best to diligently attempt to follow a path that leads toward this dream manifesting itself, but it never does. Suppose your belief systems are sound, and you actually feel like you possess the necessary specialized skills, and yet you are met with nothing but resistance, rejection, and struggle. How long do you keep chopping away at it? Do you continue on indefinitely? Or at some point, do you give up, throw a blanket over the dream and start driving for Uber twelve hours a day? You have to drive twelve hours a day, every day, because it takes that long to earn enough dough to almost pay all the bills. And when you get home, sore and exhausted, you know exactly why you only barely have enough energy to heat up a little cheap, frozen supper for yourself and pass out on the couch—as the laundry piles up into an insidious miniature mountain in the closet....

Maybe, every once in a while, as the dirty laundry moans out its unclean, wanton song, you wake up suddenly at 3:00 a.m. Sleepless, you brew a pot of coffee, whip off the blanket, and dive back into the dream. Why? Because the dream demands attention. It never truly sleeps. It lays restlessly under the dusty blanket, always at least half awake with one eye open, yearning to be loved. Not unlike the laundry in the closet, it can only be forgotten for so long. You know you can't ignore it forever.

CHAPTER 17

THE POT

JUST AFTER THE WHOLE *ROUNDERS* debacle had excruciatingly played out over the course of its drawn-out and fruitless decade, my nutty Uncle Tricky came to visit me in Redondo Beach. He thought he could cheer me up, I suppose.

Tricky showed up one day out of the blue and, much to the dismay of my neighbors, moved into my garage for two months. The garage was actually pretty pimping and just about perfectly suited to Tricky's taste and needs. Even prior to his arrival, I had already turned it into a rudimentary indoor/outdoor clubhouse. There was a couch that reclined, a coffee table, a functioning full-sized refrigerator, and a microwave, and the garage door opened up to a fantastic view of the ocean. Tricky pulled a small flat-screen TV out of the heaping pile of detritus that was the interior of his 1991 Mustang convertible that had all of the seats ripped out, plugged in an antenna, and boom, just like that he had multi-channel entertainment. The picture was even in high definition.

"Look, Al!" he'd holler whenever I went out there—he always called me Al—"I got Oprah in high def! And no cable bill!" I had to admit, it was a pretty comfortable setup, which explains why it was so hard to get him to leave.

One day I had to go grocery shopping, so I took Tricky with me to the local Trader Joe's. For the record, this probably wasn't the wisest move I'd ever made. Tricky's traveling companion at the time was a large, very wild and uncontrollable mountain dog he ironically called Pee-wee. Tricky always traveled with a dog. It was one of his road rat rules of the road. He was never without one, and the dog was always right by his side (except when he was off eating the neighbors' chickens or knocking over their garbage cans). So much so that Tricky wanted to bring Pee-wee to the store with us.

For the shopping trip, Tricky had fashioned a little sign out of cardboard and twine, which read, "I NEED A TWUNNY." His plan was to hang this sign around Pee-wee's neck and walk him around the strip mall parking lot. His twisted hope was that the well-heeled passers-by would read the sign, find both it and the dog cute, and slip Tricky a few bucks or possibly even the requested "twunny"—the humor of it being, I suppose, that the dog was smart enough to know what money was and how to write in English but not quite bright or educated enough to spell correctly.

Needless to say, I didn't want any part of that operation, nor did I even want the mangy mutt in my car. Luckily,

I was able to kibosh this plan, and Pee-wee remained safely at home. However, while I may have managed to adequately dodge that bullet, with Tricky, there was always another one lined up in the chamber with sights on your soul.

Tricky didn't shop like a normal person. He didn't believe in spending money on anything but gasoline. I don't know where he came up with this idea, but he was fairly committed to it, and even though he always seemed to have plenty of cabbage on him, he would only break this mantra on the rarest of occasions.

Here's a funny side note: Tricky used to keep his cash in his socks. But they weren't always tight-fitting; the elastics were often worn out, and the money wasn't folded neatly together or anything. The bills were sort of just crumpled up and shoved down in there. So when the socks would droop, the cash would fall out, giving him the appearance that he was leaking money as he walked around. The irony wasn't lost on me, believe me, but it was real. This was my uncle. My blood. And with me being the dutiful nephew, sometimes I would discreetly trail behind him, gather up the bills, and, after a little while, give them back to him. Only I wouldn't tell him they were his originally. I acted like I was just tossing him some beer money out of the goodness of my heart. "Here, Trick," I would say, "here's thirty, go get us some beer." And God bless him, he was always appreciative.

Despite his leaky socks, while Tricky may not have believed in buying anything, he definitely believed in eating. Therefore, whenever he went out, he always wore these crazy green cargo pants that were torn in places and held up with a tied rope belt. These pants had many, many pockets, more pockets than I had ever seen on one pair of pants. There must have been over "twunny" of them. In addition to the pockets, the pants were effusively and intricately hand-decorated with all sorts of bizarre, arcane symbols and drawings that Tricky himself had applied with a variety of different colored paints and markers. These bizarre, one-of-a-kind trousers were typically accompanied by an old blue football jersey that covered his slug-like torso. It bore no team name but was appropriately emblazoned with the numbers 00. This stylish ensemble was completed by a broken and dirty straw cowboy hat, a shaved head, and a countenance he wore on his face that was even crazier than the pants. He looked legitimately deranged at virtually all times, as if he had just been released—or more likely escaped—from a mental institution. People typically shy away from the obviously insane. Tricky was aware of this and played the part to the hilt.

Well, the second we walked into Trader Joe's, Tricky started stuffing his plethora of pockets with cans of smoked oysters, anchovies, clams—anything that looked appetizing to him that could be squirreled away in his kooky, billowing cargo pants. He didn't even really try to hide his behavior; he was doing it all more or less right out in the open. I, of course, was mortified. I fully expected that the store manager, followed shortly thereafter by the police, would descend upon him at any moment like a swarm of Nazi stormtroopers, and a huge scene would play out that would eventually lead to his being hauled off and incarcerated for shoplifting. But there was no point in trying to stop him. For as long as I had known him, he had never once listened to me about anything. So instead of confronting him or even acknowledging his presence, I took immediate evasive maneuvers and pushed my little red shopping cart as fast as it would go to the other side of the store, thus creating maximum separation between us. If he was going down, he was going down alone. I had to live there.

Alas, the store wasn't very big, and a few minutes later I turned a corner and ran into him again in the honey aisle. I instantly froze, but before I could spin the cart around and hightail it the other way, I was drawn into the scene and found myself unable to move. It was like I had accidentally happened upon a rare wild animal at a remote African watering hole. Only in this case, the creature's natural habitat was a South Redondo Trader Joe's.

I watched transfixed as Tricky took one of those plastic honey bears off the shelf, unscrewed the top, put it to his lips, and gulped down half of the honey right from the container. Right in the aisle. Right in front of Hawaiian-shirted employees stocking shelves, God, and everyone. I stared in shock and awe as he stood there, holding the bear-shaped plastic container, now only half full of honey. After a slight pause, which he took, I suppose, to savor his ill-gotten honey high, he walked right past me and straight over to the free coffee dispenser. He then casually held Mr. Honey Bear under the spigot and proceeded to fill him up with free coffee. After it was filled to his satisfaction, he simply walked away and nonchalantly strolled around the store, sipping genteelly from his makeshift, bear-shaped travel mug full of well-sweetened, piping hot coffee and stuffing canned goods in his pockets. Remarkably, no one seemed to notice. Or if they did, they were too frightened by his appearance to say anything.

Once he'd filled his pants to capacity, he walked right by me again as I waited in line to pay, and straight out the door, cool as a breeze, still sipping from the bear full of honey-coffee. No one said a word to him. No one batted an eye. I had never seen anything like it. It was like he had a crazy, magic invisibility cloak around him.

Some people in our society live above the law. Donald Trump. Harvey Weinstein (until recently), movie stars, rock stars, hedge fund managers, congressmen, dotcom and Bitcoin billionaires. These types of folks are not subject to the same rules and laws that you or I are subject to, assuming you are not one of these entitled few.

Sometimes, particularly recently, these individuals lose their privilege and entitlement upon being exposed for perpetrating whatever misdeeds they have been carelessly caught perpetrating, but for every one of these instances, there are assuredly millions more that go unreported and unexposed. There is no denying that certain members of our society live and/or have lived above the law. My *Rounders* court case was a good example of this.

Most of us live inside the law or in the middle of the law, meaning that we more or less must obey the rules and laws of society or risk paying dear consequences. We might get away with an insignificant infraction here and there, but on the whole, if we break the law and get caught, we get busted and wind up in trouble. Most of us don't possess the necessary amount of power, money, fame, or notoriety to wiggle our way out of sticky situations. We just have to deal with it.

Tricky, contrarily, rode the opposite end of the spectrum. He lived below the law. He was just as unaffected as the wealthy and famous by mundane rules and regulations, but he operated on the far end of the scale. He was not above the law or in the center of the law but below the law. Far below. And happy to be there.

Once back in the car, Tricky couldn't wait to show off his haul. The honey bear rested peacefully in a cup holder, still steaming, as if the poor little bear's head was on fire. Like in a cartoon.

"Look Al, I scored!" he roared. "I got smoked oysters, your favorite, and clams and olives and anchovies in mustard sauce and pâté. We're gonna have a very elegant garden party tonight, Al. Just like they do in Beverly Hills. How much you spend? One hundred? Guess how much I spent! Nothing!"

This last exclamation he dragged out and pronounced with some sort of self-adapted accent or affectation. When it came out of his mouth, it took him about ten seconds to finish the expression—the end result sounded like "Nut-tennnnnnnnnnnnnnnnnn!"

Which, funnily enough, is exactly how much I received as a result of all of our efforts in court. After one stolen script, ten years of legal battles, two absurd decisions, one law change, one California Lawyer of the Year honor, innumerable articles and editorials, and over five million dollars in legal fees generated by both sides, I got nothing. Zippo.

I was right back where I started.

CHAPTER 18

THE RAKE

LOSING THE *ROUNDERS* CASE HIT me hard. It hit me very, very hard. It had been ten long years of war and fight and strife, and I was in the right, and I knew it. The idea that we could lose had never even entered my mind, especially after Marder changed the law. The truth, I knew, would prevail. At least, I thought I knew. As it turned out, I knew nothing. When the reality hit me that it was over and we had lost, that there were no more appeals to make, I sank into a deep depression. It was like I was cruising down the road for ten years, heading toward this glorious destination that was always just a little bit further up ahead—a place where redemption and riches awaited me—and suddenly, a brick wall sprung up in the middle of the highway. The crash was devastating.

The bastards never settled or even offered to settle. I guess they knew they didn't have to. They offered me ten grand to drop it once, but I'd turned it down flat. That was it.

I know people always talk about a "rock bottom" moment. I'm not sure that's how it worked out for me precisely, but I will tell you that one night just after the case had been dismissed, I was cruising around the Bunker Hill section of Downtown Los Angeles, and the buddy I was with suggested we procure some crack. Sounded like a cool plan to me at the time, so we turned up the hill and down a very seedy side street and rolled up to a big apartment complex that was set back from the street by about fifty yards.

"Pull over here!" my buddy Matt instructed me. Already a little toasted, I whipped over to the side of the road and halfway up on the sidewalk, almost running over two very interesting-looking people. One was a tiny Chinese man, about 5'2" wearing a tan Members Only jacket, (torn) baggy tan pants, and a tan (dirty) fishing hat that had actual fishing lures stuck in it. His companion was a 6'7" black transgender sex worker who was dressed up like Carmen Miranda—towering fruit basket headpiece and everything. I kid you not. She had a midriff-baring, colorful, flowered blouse that was tied up, a matching sarong around her waist, and platform shoes that took her to nearly seven feet.

"They're holding," Matt said matter-of-factly, totally ignoring the odd couple's bizarre appearance.

"Really? How do you know?" I asked, amazed by his drug intuition, while slowly backing off of the sidewalk and onto the street.

"Trust me."

"Okay." Why not? What did I care? So I grabbed a "twunny," opened my door, and hopped out of the car.

"Can I get twenty?" I said coolly to Carmen, as if I did this all the time. "Sorry about my parking job."

"Sure, honey," she replied, like I was asking for a side of ranch at Denny's. What happened next shocked me even more than the fact that my buddy had been stone-cold correct that these two were slanging.

Carmen opened her well-lip-glossed, bright red mouth and took out two "thumbnails" from under her tongue, where she was storing them along with three or four others. She took my twenty sweetly and handed me the two wet, flat, rectangular, ten-dollar pieces of crack, pressing them into my palm. She then handed the twenty to the diminutive Chinese man, who snatched it violently and instantly took off running toward the apartment complex like he was shot out of a cannon. He crossed the fifty yards in about three seconds, threw open the door, and disappeared inside the building faster than an NFL running back. Carmen just looked at me and shrugged.

"You want anything else, honey?" she asked.

"No, thanks. I think I'm good for now, thanks," I stammered. Then I quickly folded myself back into the car, and we drove off into the night.

To smoke the crack, we went to one of our favorite spots, El Matador State Beach in North Malibu. El Matador was located just a couple miles up the road from Pepperdine. It's funny how in life you keep returning to the same spots. It's hardwired, I think. Like salmon swimming upstream to spawn.

Back in the day, this was a secret, hidden spot that nobody but us really knew about or ever frequented. Of course, nowadays, like all the other cool little secret spots, it's been discovered by the mass populous, and the small parking lot is always full. But then, it was just us in the lot, no other cars and no meters, and the beach was ours and ours alone. On this particular stretch of the coast, you parked above the beach on PCH and descended down a long staircase to get to the sand. There was a fairly large natural rock cave down there—still is, I imagine—that you could only access at low tide and that faced the crashing surf like something out of a movie. And that's where we dented and slit our beer can to form our pipe, smoked our cigs to create the ash for the crack bed so it didn't melt through the slits in the can, and burned and inhaled those mouth-delivered thumbnails until we were as high as the stars that twinkled over the ocean in front of us.

Sometimes when I tell this story, people who have never tried it ask me what it's like to be high on crack. Now I only did it a few times over a short period, thank God. It never really got its hooks in me as it does with some people, which was lucky for me. It's an insidious, horrible drug that only makes you want more and more and more. To be honest, there's no real way to explain what it's like to be on it in words. It's something you have to experience to understand—not that I recommend it. I most certainly do not. In fact, my advice is stay far, far away. But I can tell you this: when you're on it, it's the only thing in the world that you care about. You think, as long as I have more crack, I won't ever need anything else again. You don't care about eating, sleeping, showering, family, the weather, politics, or anything. Your whole life is that pipe, that rock, and that lighter. That's where it begins and ends. It instantly robs you of your entire existence, and your brain races. I used to write entire episodes of *Seinfeld* in my head while high. But that's just me.

Not long after that beachfront crack binge, I left LA and moved up into the mountains. I wanted out of the city and pretty much out of life. I left everything I owned behind, which wasn't much, packed a bag, and took off to the High Sierras. My destination was a little town called Twin Pines, California, where I got a job at the Twin Pines Lodge. Twin Pines Lodge was a small destination resort situated on a picturesque alpine lake. The elevation of the town was 8,000 feet, and it was beautiful. The air was clean and crisp, the mountains were glorious—for my money, the High Sierras are the most mystical and mysterious mountains on Earth—and I was surrounded by the most inspirational natural wonders you could possibly imagine. I worked as a bartender, prep cook, boat renter, wood-splitter—whatever they needed. I had no ambition to do anything but work and drink, and work and drink is what I did, not just separately, but concurrently as well. That was the culture.

When I was prep cooking at the Twin Pines Lodge restaurant, which, believe it or not, was a moderately upscale-type joint, at least for the mountains, and our old buddy Matt was dishwashing—he had decided to check out of the rat race as well—the head chef, Blanch, would call us both into the kitchen about once an hour for a "safety meeting." The meeting consisted of Blanch pouring three stainless steel ramekins full of Old Crow whiskey, which we would all shoot down together. Then I would return to my job cutting small and oddly shaped food items with very sharp knives.

Admittedly, there are some people whom I've met along the way who tend to disagree with a lot of the decisions I have made in my life. When they hear me tell these types of stories, the very kind that pepper and inform this book, they usually make comments like, "You did what? You're fucking crazy! Why would you do that?" or "You went where? Why would you go there?" or "They made you do what? Why didn't you just leave?"

I really don't have great answers for them when this happens, and it happens frequently. All I can say is that in my experience, the marginalized sections of society are where you find the cornerstone truths of the human condition.

The Old Crow was in the kitchen, ostensibly, to make the whiskey sauce that was served with the prime rib. Funny thing was, we went through roughly two fifths of Old Crow a day, even if only a quarter cup of sauce was served. There was also tequila shrimp and vodka mashed potatoes on the menu. I'm not joking. They were there just in case we ran out of "Old Dirty Buzzard" as we used to call it. It was quite an operation. It's a miracle anybody ever got served anything.

I stayed up in the mountains at Twin Pines for two years before going back down and rejoining "society." But I was never really the same. Something had been taken out of me, and there was no way to replace it. It was like I was missing a rib, if your ribs were where you stored your happiness. I was now one happy rib shy. Maybe two.

The bad guys had spent over three million dollars in legal fees over the course of the case. Our side had spent over two million, and we'd walked away with nothing. Marder did okay. He got a priceless amount of press and started his own successful firm. He was a hero. The California Lawyer of the Year who had actually changed the law. I was nobody from nowhere, broke as ever and wholly unavenged. I'd like to say it took me a long time to get over it, but that would imply that I've actually gotten over it. The truth is, I really don't think I have, and I doubt I ever will.

CHAPTER 19

THE WIN

SHOW BUSINESS IS A TOUGH racket. There's no doubt about it. It's not for the weak, weary, or faint of heart. Whether you dream of becoming an actor, director, model, musician, dancer, prancer, painter, rapper, or author, such as myself, you are going to need to arm yourself. To the teeth. If you're going to go at it in any sort of serious fashion, you had better come equipped with an undying persever-ance, a skin thicker than an elephant's hide, and an absolute steadfast unwillingness to quit. No matter what. These are the facts, plain and simple. I am not a naive individual. I pretty much knew the deal when I first decided to knock on the door, so to speak. I was well aware of the wide vari-ety of dangers and difficulties I would be forced to face on my quest for literary fortune and glory. Or at least I thought I was....

Like a lot of things, no matter how hard you think it will be, it's ten times, or a hundred times, or maybe even a thousand or a million or a zillion times harder than you could have possibly imagined. At least that has been my personal experience. I knew it was going to be tough. I knew there were going to be obstacles to overcome. I just didn't think it was going to be *this* tough or that there would be *so many* stinking obstacles. Or that they would be so seemingly insurmountable.

I have been persistently pursuing the dream of becoming a published author for over twenty years with nothing but heartbreak and tears to show for it thus far. My latest attempt to crack the code is this book you see before you now. If you are reading it in any sort of semi-legitimately published form, it must mean that my luck has changed. God willing.

On a positive tip, I recently had my first real breakthrough in a long time. Maybe not a breakthrough per se so much as a forward step in the right direction. Which is enough. I somehow actually managed to schedule an actual lunch meeting with an actual bona fide executive editor who worked for an actual bona fide publishing company. The meeting took place at an actual bona fide Mexican restaurant called Javier's that was located in an actual bona fide, obscenely opulent, endlessly sprawling behemoth of a shopping mall in Century City, CA.

This mall was something else, let me tell you. I got lost several times, and I'm not someone who normally gets lost, at least not in shopping malls. It was open air to the outdoors, had three or four levels (I'm not even sure how many), and was arranged in an asymmetrical fashion that made it tricky to navigate. There were natural wood carved chairs and benches and padded platforms of all kinds suspended from the ceilings on chains, where one could take a load off in between bouts of conspicuous consumption. There were all kinds of giant, Jurassic-type flora and fauna randomly displayed in huge pots in the walkways and store entrances, among all sorts of other strange sculptures, artwork, and fountains. Every store was seemingly opened solely for a Kardashian, and every patron looked like a model, movie star, or wannabe. I felt like I was going to get arrested just walking around, and I hadn't even done anything.

I was an hour early for the meeting, of course, and after a couple of spins around the wide Gucci corridors and a few wrong turns, I decided to play it safe and just wait in the restaurant. I took a seat at the bar, ordered an eighteen-dollar house margarita, and soaked in the scene. The first one went down so smoothly, I ordered another. As I was halfway through my second, starting to feel a little bit looser than when I had arrived, I spied a party checking in at the hostess desk who looked like they fit the bill. It was three attractive and well-dressed females, one in about her mid-thirties and two seemingly still in their early twenties. They were all well-draped in fine-fitting power suits, and from the body language they displayed, my gut told me that these were my peeps. It turned out that they were. After a moment, I grabbed my salted rim cocktail and joined them at a table in the rear of the restaurant.

This editor lady, accompanied by her two proteges, was yet another distant relative of my "manager" Barney's–

this time a third cousin on his father's side—and was only cajoled into meeting me by the fact that she felt some sort of familial obligation stemming from a Christmas holiday party she had promised to attend but did not, or something along those lines. Well, I didn't care what the impetus was behind it or where the familial guilt leverage stemmed from; I was happy just to be there. She was a legitimate editor for a well-known publishing house here in Los Angeles, and it was a coup to even get this meeting. No doubt.

Joining Sandy, the editor lady I was there to meet, were two of the prettiest girls I had ever seen in my life. They couldn't have been a day over twenty years old, and both looked like they had just walked off the cover of *Vogue*. These were Sandy's assistants, Tammy and Taylor. It was their job to read the manuscripts that were submitted to the publishing company and write critiques of them, thus informing Sandy, the executive editor, which books were worth sending toward publication and which weren't. These critiques, in addition to providing a "recommend" or "do not recommend" summation, also included notes and suggestions for the author on how that particular book could be improved. They had both kindly already done this for me, and I found their comments to be thoughtful, insightful, and well-drawn. Unfortunately, although they had said some nice, positive things about it and singled out certain sections that they enjoyed, they did not recommend my book, this book, for immediate publication. Can you believe it? However, as a happy side note, they did both say they would recommend it if I would be willing to continue to work on it, which wasn't bad, even if I didn't particularly cotton to that initial critique at first.

One of the notes I received live and in person during the lunch meeting was that the book needed more dialogue.

"Really?" I questioned.

"Yes," they all agreed. "What you have there now is great. We'd just like to see more of it."

"Okay, sure," I replied. "I can do that. I'm doing it right now. It's writing itself."

They all looked at me a bit strangely, but even so, I was feeling pretty good about things after that, at least for a brief moment. That little bit of niceness was evidently enough praise for one meeting, as Sandy chose this time to launch right into her own critique. It wasn't pretty. She had evidently also read the latest draft, which was a victory in and of itself, granted, but her liking and endorsing it was another matter entirely.

"It needs to be longer," she said. "If you walk into a bookstore and go to the nonfiction section, the average length is three hundred pages."

"Three hundred pages?!" I yelped, choking on a bite of chips and salsa. "That sounds more like a doorstop than a book. People have short attention spans these days. That seems a bit excessive, don't you think?"

She glared at me like I was an imbecile. But I continued, undaunted. "*The Great Gatsby* and *Fear and Loathing in Las Vegas*, two of my all-time favorite books, are roughly fifty thousand words, around one hundred eighty pages. So that was kind of my benchmark," I countered.

She totally ignored my rebuttal and carried on with her instructions.

"It needs to follow a proper structure. It needs to have a beginning, a middle, and an end. This is something I tell all my other writers."

"Your other writers are all hacks," I responded insolently.

My pre-meeting "take-the-edge-off" adult beverages seemed to have worked, maybe a little too well. When I heard the word "hacks" come out of my mouth, I thought to myself, *Damn, those are some strong margaritas....* I knew I wouldn't stay out of trouble for long. I never do.

"Look, I'm an outlaw," I went on, unable to stop the tequila-fueled express. "I make my own rules. I don't follow fashion..." then I started to talk-sing, in the immortal words of Adam Ant, "...that would be a joke. You know I'm gonna set them, set them. And everyone can take note, take note...." At which point I remember thinking, *Man, I need to find out what brand of tequila that bartender used... that's some good stuff.* I kept going. I was on a roll....

"Wouldn't you rather be involved with something revolutionary rather than follow a tired, old formula? I want this book to snap, crackle, and pop. I want it to sizzle like a steak on a hot grill on the Fourth of July. I want to break new ground, give them something they've never seen before. I want it to be a paper circus. I want to be the P.T. Barnum of nonfiction narrative. Three rings and a freak show...."

Sandy, bless her heart, acted like I hadn't said anything at all. Without missing a beat, she followed through with her mantra. "Beginning, middle, end," she repeated patiently. "Something happens, this leads to something else happening, A to B to C. And then there needs to be a third act denouement to sum everything up."

This actually seemed reasonable enough, but I honestly thought I had already done that.

"It has that already, no?" I argued. "It has a beginning, middle, and an end. And a denouement. And then some. I've got denouement coming out of my ears."

She wordlessly dismissed this comment and looked at me like I was a waiter who had already been given a complete order but was still for some odd reason standing by the table. Suddenly, I snapped out of it and realized that this lovely and forgiving professional editor, who had the power to make me or break me, and who was kind enough to meet with me, was just trying to be helpful. I should just shut up and be thankful. Sometimes you need to get out of your own way, difficult as it may be.

"But, of course," I back-pedaled furiously, "at the end of the day, I will do whatever you say. I want it to be published. I will follow orders. Word for word. Line for line. I will be your slave. I will come to your house and wash your car. I will clean your gutters. Anything you want."

"Don't say *anything*," she replied flirtatiously, twinkle in her eye. This lady was stone-cold cool. I dug it. It was immensely refreshing. She smiled and turned to the models/assistants. "Jeff actually tried to cancel this meeting, you know," she informed Tammy and Taylor. Then she turned to me. "Bad boy," she happily admonished. They chuckled.

This was true. After I received the assistant's initial reviews and realized that they still wanted me to do more work on the book, I had a brief bout of temporary insanity and decided to call it all off, but I had instantly regretted it, changed my mind back quickly, and was deeply ashamed of my behavior. I didn't even like hearing her say it out loud. I felt like I needed another margarita. Thankfully, she was over it and laughed it off, which was remarkable enough in its own right in this day and age, especially in Hollywood, where sometimes it seems like everyone is as fragile as a baby daisy in the wind.

By this time, I had been talking up such a storm and was so enamored with the situation, I had forgotten all about my lunch. About an hour into the meeting, Taylor looked at me and said, "You haven't touched your tacos." I had been talking nonstop so fast for so long, as I figured this was my one chance to make an impression, that I hadn't taken a single bite of my food. It didn't matter. I wasn't there for the tacos. Although, toward the end, I did end up hurriedly chowing down most of them. They were delicious.

The meeting ended abruptly but positively. After some "Nice to have met you" type pleasantries were exchanged, Sandy said, "Okay, now go to work." And that was that.

But my stomach wasn't the only thing that was no longer empty by the end of that meeting. I didn't leave empty-handed, either. I was given an overstuffed taco full of the greatest commodity known to man: hope. Managing to gain access to an actual book editor from a legitimate publishing company, one who was willing to work with me, no less, provide feedback, and try to guide me toward publication, for those of you who don't know, is tantamount to winning the lottery—if the lottery required you to submit some sort of commercially viable project. It's almost impossible to do. It doesn't seem like it should be that way, but it is. It's extremely difficult, at least in my experience. It's like trying to hit a bad beat jackpot times ten, or maybe times a hundred, or maybe more.

Now, I didn't technically have any kind of deal or contract at this point, nor even the promise of one, and there was no guarantee that I ever would. She wasn't fast-tracking my book toward publication or anything remotely close to that, but she was talking to me, and that was enough for now. That was a lot. And she was encouraging, which gave me hope. Hope that I was on the right track. Hope that one day before I croak, my circumstances might change. Hope that one day one of my screenplays will be produced. Hope that said screenplay will win me an Oscar, which I will refuse to accept, as I don't believe that art should be a competition. Hope that one day I will see my book, this book, on the virtual shelves of Amazon, having been properly published, its release setting off a nuclear supernova of fanfare and accolades. Hope that one day I will embark on a book tour, thus causing a riotous, lines-around-the-block turnout in every city and township I visit. Hope that my sales will be one one-hundredth the sales of Fifty Shades of fucking Grey. The promise of a new day. The promise of another chance. One more hand…. One more dance…. One more spin…. One more roll…. Hope.

CHAPTER 20

THE CASH OUT

IN 1991, JUST WHEN I was leaving the warm womb of college and venturing out into the cold, cruel world, the prize money for the World Series of Poker Tournament reached a cool one million dollars for the first time. The first-place prize for the main event, which was played over a No-limit Hold'em table, was $1 million in cash, plus a fancy gold bracelet. Even so, with such a huge prize to be won, hardly anyone had ever heard of the obscure tournament. Far from being covered by mainstream media or televised, it was virtually unknown to the populous at large. By contrast, in that same year, 1991, first-place prize money for Wimbledon, the famous and venerable tennis tournament held annually in England, was $500,000—only half of what you could win at the WSOP. Yet Wimbledon was extremely well-known, widely revered, and televised globally. I took notice of this discrepancy, and the gears started turning.

"What a great setting for a movie," I thought to myself. "And no one even knows this thing exists."

At the same time, I also noticed a major shift taking place in the card rooms. The Lowball tables and the Draw tables were starting to disappear entirely, and there were fewer and fewer Stud tables and more and more Hold'em tables. The Hold'em sections of the poker rooms were rapidly expanding, as they encroached on the real estate formerly held by the other games. Hold'em was gaining a ton of traction in the clubs, while remaining completely out of the public eye. Even folks who played poker regularly had never heard of it at that time. It was my dream, it was my goal, and it was my ambition to bring Texas Hold'em to the masses.

Is that indeed what occurred, just in a different way than I intended? Maybe. It sure seems like there's a decent argument to be made toward that end. I obviously didn't do it all by myself, but it seems plausible that I played some part in it, which is pretty heavy if you really think about it. So, be that as it may, where do we go from here? What's next?

Well, maybe the stars will align and I will be granted my day in the sun after all. You never know. Stranger things have happened. Maybe this book will be published and well-received. Maybe I will get to go on Ellen and Jimmy Kimmel to promote it. Hell, Ellen already has her own slot machine in Las Vegas. I kid you not. I've played it. You can walk up and shove in your bills and play the Ellen slot just like you're hanging out with her—she talks to you and everything—so she's apparently already gaming-centric. This story should be right up her alley. Hmmm. Maybe I will have my own slot machine one day. Dirty Dealing: The Game. I like it. Can you imagine? Line up three Pulitzer Prizes in the middle row and win the jackpot—martini glasses in all four corners and it doubles....

Maybe someone will want to turn this book into a movie someday. Who will play me? Matt Damon would certainly be the most ironic casting choice. Maybe my original *Shell Game* script will even be produced. Why not? It's already written. It may as well realize its potential. One never knows. It's impossible to predict the future, no matter how wizardly we may feel at the moment. You just never really know what's coming down the pike. That's what makes life so interesting. The future is gloriously unknowable. We all know where we've been, but that doesn't necessarily mean we know where we're going.

"Where do we go from here, now that all of the children are growing up?" I sang out loud to Mona, the black cat with white paws that was currently slinking across the living room floor the way cats do. She just looked up at me like I had gone mental and said nothing. But then again, she always looked at me that way. I was, of course, quoting the opening line from the Alan Parsons Project's pop classic "Games People Play." And people do love to play games, this is certain, but only as long as they win. Most folks have no interest in playing and losing. And if they have to cheat to win, well then, so be it. Hopefully, you aren't that kind of person. And if you are, well, it's never too late to change.

Personally, I have never cheated at a game in my life. I'm not claiming to be any kind of saint, but I just never saw the point. Like, why play if you're going to cheat? How is that fun? How is that even a game? It's not. It's just one asshole trying to feel superior to somebody else. For what reason, I have no idea. It seems to me that cheating would negate the whole joy of winning. How can you feel good about yourself? How can you look at yourself in the mirror? How can you sleep at night? Beats me. But it happens every minute of every day, this I can assure you. Show me a game, any game of any kind, anywhere in any land, and I'll show you someone cheating, especially in Hollywood and the surrounding area. Around here, cheating is a way of life. Lying, too, which is really pretty much the same thing. You already know how I feel about lying. It never made any sense to me. It's like if you lie, you're basically erasing your own existence. What you're saying is, "I'm not cool enough to face reality, so I'll invent my own and hope everyone buys into it." If you have to lie to get through your day, you're doing something wrong.

On a more positive note, referring back to the aforementioned Alan Parsons' lyrics, some people say that writing books, or songs for that matter, is like having kids. I'm not sure if this is exactly the case, but I can see why they would say that. Both need feeding and nurturing; both feel like they are a part of you; both are hard to let go of; and both, you know for a fact, will someday have to venture out into the world and start lives of their own—lives they will live without your immediate attention or protection. Lo and behold, it seems that we have arrived at that juncture here at *Dirty Dealing*. It is bittersweet, to be sure, there are no two ways about it. It's been fun. But if we've done our jobs correctly, and I'd like to think we have, the kids will be fine. Now, it's their turn to shine, alone, in the bright sunlight, out from under the constantly looming parental shadow.

Before we go, however, we have one last issue to address. You may have noticed that there are still a lot of pages left in this book beyond this "Cash Out" section. So if this is the end of the story, what is all that? Well, those are the extra bullets. "Bullets," if you don't already know, is a slang term used in the poker world for chips, as you fire them at your opponent with intent to destroy. And it sure never hurts to have extra. In this particular case, they are little bonuses I decided to include for your edification and entertainment.

Leading off is the actual court version of the complete list of similarities that I originally wrote out and handed to Marder on that fateful day in his glass-walled, octagonal, downtown LA, Samurai skyscraper office. This way you can gauge for yourself the length and breadth of the larceny.

Next is the infamous final ruling issued by the ever-loving Judge Ferns, the ruling that dismissed the case for good and sealed the doom of my fate.

Finally, you will find the opening twenty-five pages of the *Shell Game* screenplay. No extra charge. You might get a kick out of it, should you have the time and inclination.

And there you have it. The proof is in the pudding, so they say. The time has come. A new day has dawned. Full steam ahead, and lean hard on the throttle. Damn the torpedoes and everything else. Ah yes, we're going to let the heavenly light of truth shine down upon the world in all its hard-fought, angelic glory. For we do not go gentle into that good night, oh no, not us here at *Dirty Dealing*. Not by a long shot.

And so, in the immortal words of F. Scott Fitzgerald, whose brilliance, artistry, and insight ignited within me a desire to aspire toward goals far beyond my reach, "We beat on, boats against the current, borne back ceaselessly into the past."

SIMILARITIES

THE TEXT BELOW HAS BEEN copied and pasted from the actual filed court documents.

Funnily enough, my lawyers used pretty much every word of that original document I presented to Marder at our first meeting in his Samurai office.

"I could have been a goddamned lawyer," I said to the wind more than once.

But then, why would I want to be?

Upon viewing the movie Rounders and comparing it with The Shell Game, I find the following from The Shell Game was used in Rounders:

⊕ In both films, Texas Hold'em interferes with the protagonist's studies and relationships, causes him physical violence, and threatens his life.

⊕ In both films, the protagonist chooses poker over academia.

- In both films, the protagonist loses his tuition money gambling.

- Both movies have a character named "Worm," which is not a common nickname, and I have never met a poker player by that nickname.

- Worm, the best friend in *Rounders*, has the ace of spades tattooed on his arm...

- Jack, in *The Shell Game*, has the ace of spades etched on his Zippo lighter.

- In both films, the protagonist loses all the money he has in the world in one hand of Texas Hold'em.

- In both films, in the hand where all the money he has in the world is lost, the protagonist goes "all in" with a full house and loses to a larger full house—Mike loses nines full of aces to aces full of nines (*Rounders*). Jack loses Jacks full of aces to aces full of Jacks (*The Shell Game*).

- In both films, the girlfriend is neglected for the poker table and voices her disappointment at the neglect.

- At one point in *Rounders*, Mike explains to the audience the rudimentary fundamentals of Texas Hold'em and some of the strategy.

- At one point in *The Shell Game*, Jack explains to Munchy and the audience the rudimentary fundamentals of Texas Hold'em and some of the strategy.

- *Rounders* has a scene in which Mike names the unexposed cards of a group of poker players without the players turning the cards over.

- *The Shell Game* has a scene in which Munchy names the unexposed cards of a group of poker players without the players turning the cards over.

- *Rounders* has a scene where Mike tells his professor which are the "premium" starting hands.

- *The Shell Game* has a scene where Jack explains to Munchy which are the "premium" starting hands.

- In the climactic scene in *Rounders*, Mike uses the same strategic move on Teddy KGB that we saw Johnny Chan use earlier in the film. (They both check their nut straight.)

- In the climactic scene in *The Shell Game*, Munchy uses the same strategic move on Johnny Chan that we saw Jack use earlier in the film. (They both make like they're going to muck their hands, then raise.)

- In addition to poker clubs, both films have scenes in which the two main characters play poker in a major casino card room—in *Rounders*, Mike and Worm play at the Taj Majal in Atlantic City.

- In *The Shell Game*, Jack and Munchy play at several Las Vegas casinos.

- Both films are set in the little-known subculture of high-stakes poker and poker clubs.

- Both films revolve around the specific game of Texas Hold'em.

- This is the first time in the history of movies that Texas Hold'em has been featured in a film.

- Both films have a scene in a seedy strip club. In *Rounders*, it is frequented by Grama, who works for Teddy KGB (the Russian bad guy). In *The Shell Game*, it is frequented by the Pimp's men and owned by The Pimp (British bad guy).

- Both movies concentrate on the exploits of two guys and a girl—Leads: Mike (*Rounders*), Jack (*The Shell Game*). Best Friend: Worm (*Rounders*), Munchy (*The Shell Game*). Girlfriend: Jo (*Rounders*), Jill (*The Shell Game*).

- Both movies have similar villains: the heavily accented Russian of *Rounders*, and the heavily accented Brit of *The Shell Game*.

- *Rounders* has a sexy female card club employee who comes over to Mike's house, kisses him, and offers him sex while Jo is away.

- *The Shell Game* has a sexy female card club employee who comes over to Jack's house, kisses him, and offers him sex while Jill is away.

- Both movies have a mob-connected antagonist who wears a garish jogging suit.

- In both films, the protagonist and the beautiful blonde girlfriend attend college.

- In *Rounders*, the heavily accented villain runs a prostitution ring and a poker club.

- In *The Shell Game*, the heavily accented villain runs a strip club and plays poker.

- In both films, Johnny Chan is shown playing at the World Series of Poker tournament at the Horseshoe Casino in Las Vegas as well as one other casino card room at a different time.

- Although *Rounders* makes mention of many well-known, real life poker professionals, Chan is the only one who has a role in the film.

- Chan is also the only real-life professional that appears in *The Shell Game*.

- In *Rounders*, Chan appears in exactly two separate scenes, has no lines, and does not speak.

- In *The Shell Game*, Chan also appears in exactly two separate scenes and has no lines, nor does he speak.

- In his first scene in *Rounders*, Chan plays and wins one hand of Hold'em against an opponent who has no significance or relation to the main characters and is never seen again.

- In his first scene in *The Shell Game*, Chan plays and wins one hand of Hold'em against an opponent who has no significance or relation to the main characters and is never seen again.

- In his second *Rounders* scene, Chan plays and loses one hand of poker to one of the main characters.

- In his second *Shell Game* scene, Chan plays and loses one hand of poker to one of the main characters.

- In both films, Chan represents the human personification of the unbeatable best.

- *Rounders* begins and ends with a voice-over about poker and life from the protagonist.

- *The Shell Game* begins and ends with a voiceover about poker and life from the protagonist.

- In both films, the protagonist becomes indebted to loan sharks and is threatened with violence for nonpayment of a gambling debt. In *Rounders*, Mike owes the jogging suit wearing bad guy a $7,000 gambling debt, plus juice.

- In *The Shell Game*, Jack owes the jogging suit wearing bad guy an $8,000 gambling debt, plus juice.

- In *Rounders*, Jo finds a wad of cash in Mike's pants that makes a liar out of him and gets him in big trouble.

- In *The Shell Game*, Jill finds a wad of cash in Jack's desk that makes a liar out of him and gets him in big trouble.

- Both films contain scenes in which cocaine is snorted, though drugs are not the focus of either movie.

- In the last scene of *Rounders*, Mike leaves for Las Vegas to play in the World Series of Poker tournament and face the best player in the world, Johnny Chan. This is the only poker tournament mentioned by name in the film.

- In *The Shell Game*, all three principles go to Las Vegas and become involved with the World Series of Poker tournament. Munchy faces the world's greatest player, Johnny Chan, at the final table. This is the only poker tournament mentioned by name in the film.

⊕ In the beginning of *Rounders*, Mike watches Johnny Chan win a hand of Hold'em. This scene establishes him as the greatest card player in the world.

⊕ In the beginning of *The Shell Game*, Jack watches Johnny Chan win a hand of Hold'em. This scene establishes him as the greatest card player in the world.

⊕ In *Rounders*, Mike plays a round of poker with uniformed police officers that ends in violence. The police prevail.

⊕ In *The Shell Game*, Jack plays a round of poker with uniformed police officers that ends in violence. The police prevail.

⊕ Both films have scenes where one of the main characters is cheating at Hold'em—Worm with his dealing mechanics, Munchy with the high-tech glasses.

⊕ In the end of *Rounders*, Mike is free of debt, has a large sum of cash, and is unreformed from his gambling ways.

⊕ In the end of *The Shell Game*, Jack is free of debt, has a large sum of cash, and is unreformed from his gambling ways.

⊕ In both *The Shell Game* and *Rounders*, the protagonist uses an automotive reference to describe the game of Hold'em. Jack calls it "the hot rod of poker" in *The Shell Game*, and Mike calls it "the Cadillac of poker" in *Rounders*.

⊕ In both *The Shell Game* and *Rounders*, there is talk of street loans and juice (interest) that is 5 percent per week. This is by no means a standard or universal rate.

⊕ In both films, the trouble with the loan shark starts, not by a main character borrowing money to play and LOSING at the poker table but by a main character borrowing money to play and WINNING at the table, then choosing NOT to pay back the money that he borrowed. This was an invention solely of mine, and I believe, highly unusual.

I declare under penalty of perjury under the law of the State of California that the foregoing is true and correct.

The Final Ruling

JEFFREY ALLAN GROSSO

SUPERIOR COURT OF CALIFORNIA, COUNTY OF LOS ANGELES

DATE: 07/12/06 — DEPT. 69

HONORABLE EDWARD A. FERNS, JUDGE — L. MARKMILLER, DEPUTY CLERK

HONORABLE 11-, JUDGE PRO TEM — ELECTRONIC RECORDING MONITOR

A. AYALA, C.A., Deputy Sheriff — NONE, Reporter

8:30 am BC215947

JEFF GROSSO
VS
MIRAMAX FILM CORP

Plaintiff Counsel
Defendant Counsel

NATURE OF PROCEEDINGS:

▪ MOTION BY DEFENDANTS MIRAMAX FILM CORP, SPANKY PICTURES, DAVID LEVIEN, BRIAN KOPPLEMAN AND JOEL STILLERMAN FOR SUMMARY JUDGMENT;

In this matter taken under submission on 7-7-2006, the court rules as follows.

The motion for summary judgment is granted.

Plaintiff's sole remaining cause of action is for breach of implied contract. Defendants have established that no contract existed between the plaintiff and the defendants as there was no contact between them so that a contract could have been created. Plaintiff contends that the court must infer that there was an implied contract between the defendants and plaintiff because of the similarities of plaintiff's script and the script for "Rounders" and because defendants had access to the script plaintiff submitted to Gotham Entertainment Group ("Gotham") because Gotham's principals, Patrick McDarrah and Joel Roodman, had a close business relationship with defendant Miramax Film Corporation ("Miramax"), and with the people who Miramax contends wrote the script for "Rounders", defendants David Levien and Brian Koppelman.

Plaintiff sets forth at great length the similarity of ideas used in his script for "The Shell Game" and the script for "Rounders". Those purported

Page 1 of 9 DEPT. 69

MINUTES ENTERED
07/12/06
COUNTY CLERK

08/02/06

200

SUPERIOR COURT OF CALIFORNIA, COUNTY OF LOS ANGELES

DATE: 07/12/06			DEPT. 69
HONORABLE EDWARD A. FERNS	JUDGE	L. MARKMILLER	DEPUTY CLERK
HONORABLE 11A	JUDGE PRO TEM		ELECTRONIC RECORDING MONITOR
A. AYALA, C.A.	Deputy Sheriff	NONE	Reporter

8:30 am	BC215947	Plaintiff Counsel	
	JEFF GROSSO VS MIRAMAX FILM CORP	Defendant Counsel	

NATURE OF PROCEEDINGS:

similarities between the scripts have already been
determined insufficient to establish a claim for
copyright infringement, however, no court has
foreclosed plaintiff from attempting to establish
that there was an agreement with the defendants to
pay for the use of an idea. Thus, in the instant
case, this court must determine whether or not there
was a promise to pay for an idea if the idea was used
by the defendants, and whether or not the idea was
used.

The court overrules the objections to plaintiff's
characterizations of the idea in the scripts and
accepts as true for the purpose of this motion that
plaintiff has observed both works, and has determined
that many of the same ideas are found in both works.
This court also accepts as true that the date
plaintiff submitted his script to Gotham and its
principals, and the date Levien and Koppelman
submitted their screenplay to defendant Joel
Stillerman at defendant Spanky Pictures, are so close
in time that some inference may be made that some of
the ideas expressed in both works may have had a
common host.

Even accepting plaintiff's evidence as admissible,
plaintiff has failed to raise a triable issue of fact
as to whether or not an agreement may be implied from
any of the defendants' conduct. An implied agreement
consists of obligations arising from a mutual
agreement and intent to promise where the agreement

08/02/06

Page   2 of   9   DEPT. 69

MINUTES ENTERED
07/12/06
COUNTY CLERK

●   ●

SUPERIOR COURT OF CALIFORNIA, COUNTY OF LOS ANGELES

DATE: 07/12/06				DEPT. 69
HONORABLE EDWARD A. FERNS	JUDGE	L. MARKMILLER		DEPUTY CLERK
HONORABLE 11*8*	JUDGE PRO TEM			ELECTRONIC RECORDING MONITOR
A. AYALA, C.A.	Deputy Sheriff	NONE		Reporter

8:30 am	BC215947	Plaintiff Counsel	
	JEFF GROSSO VS MIRAMAX FILM CORP	Defendant Counsel	

NATURE OF PROCEEDINGS:

and promise have not been expressed in words. <u>See</u>, <u>Desny v. Wilder</u> (1956) 46 C.2d 715, 734; 299 P.2d 257. In other words, the implied-in-fact contract must have the essential elements of mutual assent and consideration.

Here, plaintiff's own evidence shows that any promise made to him to pay for an idea was made by Gotham through its principals, and not by any of the named defendants in this action. Plaintiff has not established an evidentiary link between Gotham's acceptance of his script for review, and an enforceable promise by any of the named defendants. Even if the principals at Gotham mentioned plaintiff's ideas to employees and agents of Miramax or to employees or agents of Spanky, there is no evidence that any of the defendants knew of the original source of the idea, and any agreement by Gotham to pay for an idea. Plaintiff's entire premise is based upon the speculation as to the evolution of an idea, and not upon an agreement made by any defendant in this action .

Finally, plaintiff contends that an agreement exists between Gotham and Miramax, under which plaintiff is a third party beneficiary and/or Gotham was acting as Miramax's agent. Plaintiff's theories are based upon speculation derived from publications which inform that Gotham has some sort of a "deal" with Miramax, and, the purported similarity between the ideas in "Rounders" and plaintiff's work. Again, the

Page   3 of   9   DEPT. 69

08/02/06

SUPERIOR COURT OF CALIFORNIA, COUNTY OF LOS ANGELES

ATE: 07/12/06			**DEPT.** 69
)NORABLE EDWARD A. FERNS	JUDGE	L. MARKMILLER	DEPUTY CLERK
)NORABLE 1C	JUDGE PRO TEM		ELECTRONIC RECORDING MONITOR
A. AYALA, C.A.	Deputy Sheriff	NONE	Reporter

8:30 am	BC215947	Plaintiff Counsel	
	JEFF GROSSO VS MIRAMAX FILM CORP	Defendant Counsel	

NATURE OF PROCEEDINGS:

similarity in works does not establish a contract
because it does not establish the existence of a
contract.   Plaintiff has not provided an agreement
between Gotham and Miramax, only speculation that
some sort of agreement existed.

In order to establish that plaintiff was a third
party beneficiary of an agreement, plaintiff must
show the contract was made expressly for plaintiff's
benefit.   Civil Code § 1559.

Plaintiff has not established the existence of a
contract, the terms of any agreement, or any
expressed intent by Miramax or an agent of Miramax to
benefit the plaintiff.   Plaintiff has not identified
any contract under which Miramax retained Gotham as
an agent.   The contract which plaintiff contends
creates an agency was not provided by the plaintiff,
but was provided by the defendants in the reply.
This court may not consider evidence submitted in a
supplemental declaration in the reply papers for the
purpose of establishing defendants' initial burden of
proof.   San Diego Watercrafts, Inc. v. Wells Fargo
Bank, N.A. (2002) 98 Cal.App.4th 1316, 1320.   This
court considers the document in support of
plaintiff's argument, but not in support of
defendants' burden.   Again, defendants met their
burden in their initial papers.

The March 27, 1995, contract submitted by defendants
does not contain an express agreement to pay a person

Page   4 of   9   DEPT. 69

DATE: 07/12/06	DEPT. 69
HONORABLE EDWARD A. FERNS JUDGE	L. MARKMILLER DEPUTY CLERK
HONORABLE 11D JUDGE PRO TEM	ELECTRONIC RECORDING MONITOR
A. AYALA, C.A. Deputy Sheriff	NONE Reporter

8:30 am BC215947

JEFF GROSSO
VS
MIRAMAX FILM CORP

Plaintiff
Counsel

Defendant
Counsel

NATURE OF PROCEEDINGS:

who has submitted a screenplay to Gotham. Under the
agreement, Miramax agrees to "an exclusive 'First
Look/Last Matching Right' acquisition/distribution
deal whereby [Gotham is] obligated to submit to
Miramax on a 'First Look' and 'Last Matching Right'
basis all projects you own, control or represent or
desire to acquire and/or distribute in any and all
media." The agreement was in effect from April 1,
1995, to April 1, 1996. Miramax contends the
agreement expired on April 1, 1996. Plaintiff
contends that it did not expire for 90 days after
April 1, 1996, and that his work was a project
submitted pursuant to the agreement.

Even assuming his work was submitted during the term
of the contract, plaintiff has not established that
he was an intended beneficiary. A third party may
enforce a contract expressly for the benefit of that
party. Civil Code § 1559. The contract need not be
exclusively for the benefit of the third party and
the third party need not be named or identified in
the contract. COAC, Inc. v. Kennedy Engineers(1977)
67 Cal.App.3d 916, 919-920. "Insofar as intent to
benefit a third person is important in determining
his right to bring an action under a contract, it is
sufficient that the promisor must have understood
that the promisee had such intent...No specific
manifestation by the promisor of an intent to benefit
the third person is required. Lucas v. Hamm (1961)
56 Cal.2d 583, 591.

Page 5 of 9 DEPT. 69

MINUTES ENTERED
07/12/06
COUNTY CLERK

SUPERIOR COURT OF CALIFORNIA, COUNTY OF LOS ANGELES

DATE: 07/12/06		DEPT. 69
HONORABLE EDWARD A. FERNS JUDGE	L. MARKMILLER	DEPUTY CLERK
HONORABLE 11E JUDGE PRO TEM		ELECTRONIC RECORDING MONITOR
A. AYALA, C.A. Deputy Sheriff	NONE	Reporter

8:30 am	BC215947	Plaintiff Counsel
	JEFF GROSSO VS MIRAMAX FILM CORP	Defendant Counsel

NATURE OF PROCEEDINGS:

In order to determine whether the plaintiff was an
intended third party beneficiary of the contract
between Gotham and Miramax, the court is required to
determine whether Miramax objectively understood that
it was assuming an obligation to someone other than
Gotham. In the instant case, Miramax agreed to look
at projects in which Gotham was interested, however,
the contract does not express an intent by Miramax to
benefit plaintiff, or a class in which plaintiff is
shown to be a member. Under the agreement, Gotham is
to present projects that Gotham has an interest in
acquiring and distributing, and if Miramax is
interested in acquiring the screenplay, then Gotham
and Miramax must negotiate a deal in good faith.
Gotham wished to develop motion pictures, and
undertook to find those projects. Miramax agreed to
look at and evaluate submissions by Gotham. The
purpose of the contract is to enable Gotham to
develop motion pictures with the aid of Miramax, and
not for Miramax to assist third parties. Plaintiff
does not make clear why he has sought relief from
Miramax rather than Gotham and/or its principals,
however, even if plaintiff chooses not to name the
party who invited him to submit his screenplay,
plaintiff may not ignore Gotham's obligations under
the contract, and impose the obligations on Miramax
in its stead.

Plaintiff has not established that there was an
agency relationship, actual or ostensible, between
Miramax and Gotham.

Page   6 of   9   DEPT. 69

MINUTES ENTERED
07/12/06
COUNTY CLERK

SUPERIOR COURT OF CALIFORNIA, COUNTY OF LOS ANGELES

DATE: 07/12/06			DEPT. 69
HONORABLE EDWARD A. FERNS	JUDGE	L. MARKMILLER	DEPUTY CLERK
HONORABLE 11F	JUDGE PRO TEM		ELECTRONIC RECORDING MONITOR
A. AYALA, C.A.	Deputy Sheriff	NONE	Reporter

| 8:30 am | BC215947 | Plaintiff Counsel | |
| | JEFF GROSSO VS MIRAMAX FILM CORP | Defendant Counsel | |

NATURE OF PROCEEDINGS:

There was no actual agency under the agreement. Civil Code § 2299 provides that "[a]n agency is actual when the agent is really employed by the principal." In the instant case, the subject agreement is not one which provides that Gotham is to represent Miramax in obtaining screenplays. The agreement provides merely that Miramax will assess projects which Gotham submits to it.

There was also no ostensible agency. Civil Code § 2300 provides that "[a]n agency is ostensible when the principal intentionally, or by want of ordinary care, causes a third person to believe another to be his agent who is not really employed by him." "Ostensible authority is such as a principal, intentionally or by want of ordinary care, causes or allows a third person to believe the agent to possess." Civil Code § 2317. Miramax did not make any representations to plaintiff, and the publications which concern the "deal" between Miramax and Gotham do not contain language which would lead anyone to reasonably believe that Miramax had made Gotham its agent for the purpose of purchasing screenplays. Moreover, the publications have not been shown to be the result of some act or conduct on the part of Miramax.

CLERK'S CERTIFICATE OF MAILING/
NOTICE OF ENTRY OF ORDER

Page   7 of   9   DEPT. 69

MINUTES ENTERED
07/12/06
COUNTY CLERK

08/02/06

SUPERIOR COURT OF CALIFORNIA, COUNTY OF LOS ANGELES

DATE: 07/12/06			DEPT. 69
HONORABLE EDWARD A. FERNS	JUDGE	L. MARKMILLER	DEPUTY CLERK
HONORABLE 11*G*	JUDGE PRO TEM		ELECTRONIC RECORDING MONITOR
A. AYALA, C.A.	Deputy Sheriff	NONE	Reporter

8:30 am	BC215947		
	JEFF GROSSO	Plaintiff Counsel	
	VS MIRAMAX FILM CORP	Defendant Counsel	

NATURE OF PROCEEDINGS:

I, the below named Executive Officer/Clerk of the above-entitled court, do hereby certify that I am not a party to the cause herein, and that this date I served Notice of Entry of the above minute order of 7-12-2006 upon each party or counsel named below by depositing in the United States mail at the courthouse in Los Angeles, California, one copy of the original entered herein in a separate sealed envelope for each, addressed as shown below with the postage thereon fully prepaid.

Date: 7-12-2006

John A. Clarke, Executive Officer/Clerk

By: _____ *L. Markmiller* _____
L. MARKMILLER

John A. Marder
Michele L. Levinson
MANNING & MARDER
KASS, ELLROD, RAMIREZ LLP
23rd Floor at Figueroa Tower
660 S. Figueroa Street
Los Angeles, CA 90017

Page 8 of 9 DEPT. 69

MINUTES ENTERED
07/12/06
COUNTY CLERK

SUPERIOR COURT OF CALIFORNIA, COUNTY OF LOS ANGELES

DATE: 07/12/06			DEPT. 69
HONORABLE EDWARD A. FERNS	JUDGE	L. MARKMILLER	DEPUTY CLERK
HONORABLE 11ℋ	JUDGE PRO TEM		ELECTRONIC RECORDING MONITOR
A. AYALA, C.A.	Deputy Sheriff	NONE	Reporter

8:30 am	BC215947	Plaintiff Counsel	
	JEFF GROSSO		
	VS	Defendant	
	MIRAMAX FILM CORP	Counsel	

NATURE OF PROCEEDINGS:

Louis P. Petrich
Robert S. Gutierrez
LEOPOLD, PETRICH & SMITH, P.C.
2049 Century Park East
Suite 3110
Los Angeles, CA 90067

Page 9 of 9 DEPT. 69

MINUTES ENTERED
07/12/06
COUNTY CLERK

08/02/06

THE SHELL GAME SCREENPLAY

THE SHELL GAME

by
Jeffrey Allan Grosso

34 Eleventh Court
Hermosa Beach, CA
90254

THE SHELL GAME

Three friends discover that getting rich quick can be dangerous business.

The Shell Game is a story about money and the people who want it. Choosing to forsake the straight and narrow path for the exciting but unpredictable world of Southern California card clubs, Jack Baker, a gifted but irresponsible college student, finds himself cornered by his own recklessness and decides to take a desperate shot at instant salvation.

On route to meet his impishly clever roommate Munchy and angelically sinful girlfriend Jill in glittering Las Vegas, Jack by chance encounters an all too familiar loan shark and his crime boss employer. Meanwhile, Jill manages to attract the attention of a trigger-happy, British nobleman turned Las Vegas pimp.

The shells start to move as Jack's debt and Jill's charm splits the trio into two groups who each become embroiled in separate, subversive plots to steal the million dollars in prize money for the richest poker tournament in history, "The World Series of Poker".

All parties collide amidst the mayhem of the famous tournament and a mad scramble for the cash ensues, spilling blood all around. Just as the three friends are about to be added to the growing body count, Jack performs the greatest trick of all and engineers their escape with double the prize money turning the weekend excursion into an adventure the three of them will never forget.

FADE IN: EXT. DUSK. Las Vegas boulevard, otherwise known as
The Strip. The sun is setting behind the mountains.

VOICE OVER:

> JACK
> Some people say that poker is
> the sport of kings.

CUT TO: Excalibur hotel

> JACK
> Other people claim that poker
> is the sport of thieves.

CUT TO: The Jolly Roger Treasure Island sign.

> JACK
> And there's at least one guy
> who'll try and tell you that
> the game of poker is the game
> of life.

CUT TO: The MGM lion, bronze dolphin, flaming, golden
horse and chariot.

> JACK
> Then there's the people who
> think that poker is just
> another card game. I used to
> be one of those people.

CUT TO: Five feet away from the South side of the Luxor
hotel. Shiny, smooth blackness.

> JACK
> Then one day I tried a game
> called Texas Hold'em.

The CAMERA RISES to offer a view of the Strip.

                    JACK
          It seemed like a harmless
          enough idea at the time.

The lights of the strip come on from North to South. The
end of the VOICE OVER and the start of the MUSIC ignite the
beacon that shines up from the peak of the pyramid.

                    JACK
          Who knew?

CUE MUSIC: "ANYTHING" by DRAMARAMA

CUT TO: The back entrance to the Hollywood Park Casino in
Inglewood, CA. It is a cement stoop and stairs with a pay
phone. There are two patrons making a deal and a nervous
dealer smoking.

ESTABLISH JIMMY: Half Mexican, Half Asian dealer. Short
and slight with coifed hair.

The back door opens and ROCCO walks out.

ESTABLISH ROCCO: Dim-witted but capable henchman with no
neck.

ROCCO looks at the dealmakers and they flee. JIMMY panics.

                    ROCCO
          Hi Jimmy, how are you feeling?

JIMMY looks over the railing. ROCCO grabs his neck.

                    ROCCO
          You look a little haggard
          Jimmy, have you been getting
          enough rest? Why don't we go
          for a walk, get the blood
          circulating.

They head behind the giant air filtration unit. JIMMY
makes a break for it. ROCCO catches him and throws him to
the ground.

                    ROCCO
          Now don't be rude Jimmy, we
          haven't finished our
          conversation. I still have an
          unresolved issue to discuss
          with you.

ROCCO kicks him in the mid-section.

                    ROCCO
          I hope this doesn't upset you
          because I like you Jimmy, I
          really do. I think you have a
          lot of good qualities.

He kicks him again

                    ROCCO
          But punctuality doesn't seem to
          be one of them. And as luck
          would have it, one of my
          weaknesses happens to be in the
          area of patience.

On "patience" ROCCO kicks him again, then crouches down and
grabs him by the hair.

                    ROCCO
          Now normally in a situation
          like this I would simply break
          a couple fingers or a thumb
          and that would be the end of
          it. But since you are
          currently employed as a card
          dealer…

ROCCO smashes his face into the cement.

                    ROCCO
          And since I wish to support
          you in your choice of
          occupation…

He smashes his face again.

> ROCCO
> I'm gonna leave your dainty,
> little fingers alone.

ROCCO smashes his face one last time and stands up.

> ROCCO
> But I suggest, if you don't
> wish to have any more of these
> little chats, that you make a
> better effort to fulfill your
> responsibilities.

On the last half of "responsibilities" ROCCO kicks him one
more time.

> ROCCO
> I knew you'd understand. Have
> a nice day.

ROCCO departs.

CUT TO: INT. DAY Disaster of a dorm room, Pepperdine
University. Malibu, CA. This is the source of the MUSIC.

ESTABLISH JACK BAKER: Twenty-something college student.
Athletic. Dreamer. Schemer. Disorganized and
irresponsible but smart and creative.

ESTABLISH RUDY "MUNCHY" JOHNSON: Shorter, more comical
and more animated than JACK. Disheveled appearance all the
time. Undeclared major. JILL's fraternal twin brother.

CUT TO: JACK and MUNCHY are seated facing each other on
the unmade bed. Both are drinking beer.

CUE MUSIC: "LIFE DURING WARTIME-TAKE ME TO THE RIVER" -
THE TALKING HEADS.

JACK is shuffling and manipulating a deck of cards.

> JACK
> Let's start right at the top.
> Texas Hold'em, the hot rod of
> poker games.

CUT TO: INT. NIGHT. Hollywood Park. EXTREME CLOSE UP of someone (JACK) snorting a line of coke off a toilet paper dispenser in a bathroom stall.

CUT TO: INT. Dorm room.

> MUNCHY
> Wait a minute, you sure we
> should get into this now? We
> got Econ in five minutes.

CUT TO: The TV with no volume. The cartoon where Daffy has infiltrated the cache of Ali Babba and is wheeling out the treasure in a huge cart.

> JACK
> Econ? Are you kidding me? I
> can give you a whole semester
> of that shit right here in two
> minutes.

JACK makes himself a Bloody Mary with everything. He drinks it down in one swig and makes another. He is flipping channels on the TV. He switches to an infomercial for the tummy-buster. Then to "This Old House". Bob Villa is restoring an old mansion.

> JACK
> There's only three things you
> need to know about Economics.
> First, people have unlimited
> wants, that's a given.

He flips to a girl in a car gazing up at the Marlborough billboard on Sunset Blvd. She presses in her cigarette lighter.

> JACK
> And they never forget any of

them because they're constantly
being reminded of the things
they don't have.

He flips to a commercial for Pringles, then Diet Coke, then
a Franklin Mint collection of model cars.

                    JACK
          TV commercials are ruining this
          country. Millions of Americans
          sit in front of the box all day
          munching on potato chips,
          slugging down cases of diet
          soda, and they drool caramel
          coloring over everything they
          see. The ad guys make the stuff
          look so good, and the people are
          so gullible and materialistic,
          they even want the shit from the
          Franklin Mint.

                    MUNCHY
          You're kidding.

                    JACK
          I'm not.

JACK flips to a news story about postal workers. A mailman
is depositing a stack of junk into a mailbox. It won't all
fit. There is a long row of overstuffed mailboxes.

                    JACK
          Then they get a bazillion
          catalogues in the mail with
          more shit they can't live
          without.

JACK flips to CNN "Moneyline." A sheet of credit cards
comes off an assembly line. He flips to cartoon. A bomb
lands on DAFFY. He flips to the Weather Channel. JACK
tosses the remote to MUNCHY.

                    JACK
          This constant multimedia
          blitzkrieg keeps building and
          building until the people

can't stand it anymore, and
they just explode into a giant
mushroom cloud of shredded
American Express cards that
fills up the whole sky and
blocks out the rays of the sun
for a thousand years.

MUNCHY flips to a commercial for Jeep. A new Grand Cherokee
in a driveway with a bow on it. A daughter hugs her
father.

> JACK
> So rule number one is everybody
> wants everything all the time,
> and they want it with the gold
> trim sport package, and they
> want it gift wrapped with a big
> red bow on top, and they want it
> right now, and then in a week
> they want a new one. Which
> brings us to rule number two.

He flips to a huge wall of televisions playing a Lexus
commercial. Then a bulldozer plowing through an
overflowing landfill.

JACK walks to the bathroom with his drink. He urinates,
still talking. The bathroom is papered with LA Express
pages and prostitution flyers from Las Vegas. One section
is mock-ups of hundred dollar bills with nubile babes in
lieu of dead presidents. They are old and falling down.

MUNCHY flips to Sanford and Son. Fred is tossing his bills in
the trash.

> JACK
> The problem is the world has
> a limited number of resources
> that can't keep up with our
> unlimited wants.

MUNCHY flips to a Lotto drawing. Then to the stands at
a race track. Then to the CNN stock report.

> JACK

That's why people gamble.   I
don't care if it's dog races,
mutual funds, quick six picks,
pork belly futures…

JACK flushes and returns.

> JACK
> Or throwing dice up against
> the wall of an alley.

MUNCHY flips to "I Dream Of Jeanie."

> JACK
> They all want the same thing.
> They want to magically turn
> their limited resources into a
> good luck genie who will
> mystically rise out of a barrel
> of ping-pong balls, or fly out
> of the ass of a three year old
> quarter horse, and satisfy all
> of their personal wants for
> ever and ever.

MUNCHY flips to the "The Love Boat," then throws the
remote. It lands on top of the TV remote and the TV turns off.

> JACK
> That's the fantasy.   And
> that's where we come in. And
> we're ready for them. Do you
> know why?

> MUNCHY
> Rule number three.

> JACK
> Exactly.   Which is?

JACK takes a hit from the bong which has been customised.

          MUNCHY
No animal shall sleep in a
bed. No wait, wrong class...
I got it, supply and demand.

          JACK
Correct, Doctor Munch.
Here's how it works. Eight or
nine jokers sit down at a
poker table and supply the
game with cash money. Then we
sit down next to them and
demand that they give it to
us.

          MUNCHY
That sounds easy.

          JACK
It is. But there's a trick to it.
You've got to win. And in order
to win you've got to have the
best hand. Or you've got to make
the other guys think you have
the best hand. If you make a
bet and everybody folds, then
you win no matter what. You
could have the worst fucking
hand ever dealt in the history
of the great game of poker, but
since you had the balls to bet,
and nobody called you. you win
anyway. That's called bluffing.

          MUNCHY
How do you know when to bluff?

          JACK
Well, that's the real trick,
isn't it. And it's going to
cost you something extra.

CUT TO: EXT DAY. Inglewood. A drug deal on the corner of
Prairie and Century. CLOSE UP of the drug dealer and
customer (JACK) making the exchange.

CUT TO INT.

> MUNCHY
> Rule number four, put it on
> my tab.

CUT TO EXT. After the deal, JACK walks down the block and
across the street.

CUT TO INT.

> JACK
> Very good. You should work in
> Washington. So do you want to
> learn how to play or what?

> MUNCHY
> What about Banks' class? If
> we ditch again he's gonna
> dock us half a grade point
> average or something.

CUT TO EXT. Once he crosses, JACK walks down a sidewalk
with a fence. He turns left into a driveway entrance. He
takes a few steps and stops.

CUT TO INT.

> JACK
> Fuck it, let him. I'm sick
> of taking out loans to sit
> through boring three hour
> classes. School costs money,
> I'm talking about making
> money, and you don't need a
> fucking sheepskin hanging on
> the wall to do it. There's
> millions of dollars running
> by all the time out there,
> just like this river of
> money. All you gotta do is
> lean over and dip in your
> bucket.

CUT TO EXT. JACK's SHOES. He is standing in a flower
lined patch of grass. We hear a waterfall close by.

                    MUNCHY
          What if you lean over too far,
          fall in, and get swept away by
          the ferocious current?

CUT TO: JACK stares at MUNCHY, then hands him his drink.
JACK leaps on the bed in a surfer's stance. He waves his
hand next to his head pretending to be in the curl.

FADE OUT.

FADE IN: A large auditorium lecture class. The teacher is
calling roll.

                    TEACHER
          Baker......Baker...

CUT TO: MARK and JILL sitting next to each other in the
auditorium. MARK has ten notebooks and three pens.

ESTABLISH JILL: (Alicia Silverstone) Blondish,
wholesomely beautiful girl next door. MUNCHY's   Has
been seeing JACK for a few months.   sister.

ESTABLISH MARK: Semi-nerdy, accounting major. Measures
his life in coffee spoons. Parties under peer pressure. In
love with JILL.

                    MARK
          That loser hasn't been here all
          semester. I don't see why Banks
          even bothers to call his name
          anymore.

                    JILL
          Why are you always so negative?

                    MARK
          What do you mean?

                    JILL
          Calling somebody a loser just
          because they miss an Econ class,
          you don't even know him.

                    MARK
          I know enough. You can't pass
          a class you don't show up for,

> that makes you a loser in my
> book. Where's your brother by
> the way? With the loser I bet.

              JILL
> Look who's talking. You're
> barely passing and you're here
> early every day with your ten
> volume notebook set.

              MARK
> I like to have thorough, detailed
> notes. It's important.

              JILL
> Important to who? You cheated
> off me on the last test anyway.

              MARK
> Only on a couple questions.

              JILL
> It was an essay test. There
> were only two questions on it.

MARK starts to write. The teacher is putting a pie chart
on the overhead projector.

              JILL
> What are you writing? What
> kind of crap do you have in
> there anyway, what Banks
> likes on his pizza?

              MARK
> No. Do you think we'll be
> tested on that?

CUT TO: JACK is teaching DICKY how to play Hold'em. He
puts his beer down and deals.

              JACK
> OK listen up, you're gonna be
> tested on this...Where was I?
> Oh yeah, Texas Hold'em. The
> .44 Magnum of poker games.
> OK, each player gets two
> cards face down.

JACK finishes dealing.

> JACK
> The rules are the same as
> regular poker, but in Hold'em
> you only get to hold two cards
> in your hand. Then all the
> players share the five cards
> that are spread out in the
> middle.

> MUNCHY
> Wait, I only get two cards?

> JACK
> Yea, two in your hand.

> MUNCHY
> What if they suck? Do I get
> to draw new cards?

> JACK
> No. No draw. You're stuck with
> the ones you're dealt so you
> better make sure they're good.
> That means you've got to fold
> a lot of hands right off the bat.
> A lot of people play every hand
> to the end and they go broke
> faster than we do at a craps
> table.

> MUNCHY
> Whoa.

> JACK
> That's the bad news. The good
> news is that when you finally
> decide to play a hand, you get
> to play off five more cards that
> get spread out in the middle of
> the table. Everybody plays off
> these same five cards. So you
> got seven cards total to work
> with.

> MUNCHY
> But I don't need seven spades
> to make a flush do I?

                    JACK
          No just five. Just like seven
          card stud. The cool part is
          that you can use one, or both
          of the cards in your hand, so
          if you only have one spade in
          your hand, and there's four
          spades on the board, then
          you've still got the flush.
          Got it?

                    MUNCHY
          I think so.

                    JACK
          Everybody plays off of the
          same cards in the middle and
          they're spread out in stages.
          First the dealer spreads out
          three, then you bet, this is
          called the flop.

JACK flops three cards face up. A king, deuce, and seven.

                    MUNCHY
          Why do they call it that?

                    JACK
          Cause they kind of flop it
          over. Then you bet. After
          you finish betting, the
          dealer puts out another card.
          This is called the turn card.

JACK puts another card next to the others. A five.

                    MUNCHY
          Why do...

                    JACK
          I don't know. Then you bet
          again. Then the dealer puts
          out the last card and you bet
          one more time. The last card
          is called the river card.They
          call it that because if
          you're still in at this point

you took your hand all the way
to the river.

JACK turns over a queen.

> MUNCHY
> The river of money?

> JACK
> That's right, the river of
> money.

> MUNCHY
> Is there a rope swing?

> JACK
> Is there a rope swing. Yes
> there's a rope swing, and a
> diving board, and a cooler
> full of Corona, and Kirsten
> Kirschner in a tiger striped
> bikini.

MUNCHY gets excited.

> MUNCHY
> OOOooooh.

JACK turns over his hand and matches it up with the cards
on the board.

> JACK
> If you win.

He lines up two pair, Kings and Queens.

> JACK
> But if you lose..

JACK turns over MUNCHY'S cards, he makes a pair of deuces
with a nine kicker. JACK leers at MUNCHY, who has cowered
back from his celebration.

                    JACK
              Cement shoes.

FADE OUT.

FADE IN: EXT DAY. CLOSE UP of JACK's loafers.

CUT TO: EST. SHOT: JACK is standing in a grass field at
Hollywood Park. He lights a cigarette and glances at his
watch. It is seven a.m. He has been up all night. He
checks his wallet. Eight bucks. He walks up to the
casino. The entire gamut of freaks and fools is present.
He nods to a few people on the way, then spots a weird
looking dude across the casino. It is the JUICE MAN.

ESTABLISH JUICE MAN: Low level loan shark. Asian. Short
and strange. Dressed like a nightmarish jogger.

JACK ducks in the bathroom. He re-emerges sniffling. Two
guys are walking in front of him. One dressed in Laker
gear, the other in LA Kings. One points to a stoic Asian
man playing Hold'em.

                    GUY #1
              Hey isn't that Johnny Chan?

                    GUY #2
              Yup.

                    Guy #1
              Wow. Johnny Chan, Johnny Man,
              Johnny Poker. Didn't he win
              the World Series last year?

                    Guy #2
              Yup, year before that too.
              Back to back million dollar
              paydays.

                    Guy #1
              (whistles)

                    GUY #2
              Guy is the king.

                    GUY #1
              What's he doing here? World
              Series starts this week
              doesn't it?

                    GUY #2
          Yup.

                    GUY #1
          Isn't he gonna go for the
          three-peat?

                    GUY #2
          Course he is. Guess he's
          getting in some last minute
          practice. It's only an hour
          plane ride to Vegas.

                    GUY #1
          You going?

                    GUY #2
          Are you kidding? The buy in
          is ten grand. Besides,
          who's gonna beat that guy?

They walk by his table. JOHNNY CHAN makes a large bet with
no emotion. His opponent sweats a bit, then folds.

CUT TO: JACK has now reached the JUICE MAN.

                    JUICE MAN
          Hey Big Jack. You got a
          tip for me?

JACK lights another butt.

                    JACK
          Sure. Part your hair on the
          other side. Say, how about
          flowing me half a giesel so I
          can get in a game.

                    JUICE MAN
          Ohh Jack, what happened, man?
          You lose again last night? I
          told you to change seats. You
          never listen.

                    JACK
          Yea, I'm the worst. Can I

have the cash?

                    JUICE MAN
          Ohh, I don't know, man. You
          already owe me eight thousand. It
          ain't peanuts no more. When you figure
          you'll have it back?

                    JACK
          Soon as I beat up this game
          over here.

                    JUICE MAN
          I don't know, you're running kinda
          bad, aint ya?

                    JACK
          I know I'm running bad. You
          know I'm running bad. Everybody
          in this place knows. But I can't
          run bad forever. You want your
          scratch back? Put me in a game.
          You know how long it would take me
          to save eight grand at some
          dumb day job?

                    JUICE MAN
          (curious)
          How long?

                    JACK
          Longer than you'll live.

                    JUICE MAN
          OK Big Jack, you're a good
          guy, I'll give you one more
          chance. Ok? But this is the
          last time. Understand?

ROCCO appears and nods at JIMMY walking by. The JUICE MAN
nods back. ROCCO follows JIMMY.

CUT TO: JACK looks at the JUICE MAN.

                    JUICE MAN
          I gave him last chance yesterday.

The JUICE MAN pulls out a huge wad of hundreds from his Picasso sweatsuit. He peels off five and hands them to JACK.

                    JUICE MAN
          Play good.

JACK hands his lit cig to an older lady walking by. She takes it without a glance and smokes it, still walking.

                    JACK
          (walking away)
          Our father who art in heaven,
          hallowed be thy name..

JACK heads to the top section Hold'em board. He passes scantily clad cocktail waitresses, coke dealers, gang members, and acres of flying money.

                    JACK
          Thy kingdom come, thy will be
          done on Earth as it is in
          Heaven. Give us this day, our
          daily bread, and forgive us
          our trespasses, as we forgive
          those who trespass against us,
          and lead us not into
          temptation, but deliver us from
          evil.

He arrives at the board. (waiting list) The board girl greets him.

ESTABLISH CHANTEL: Black, mid twenties.

A floor man has just whispered something in her ear as JACK approaches. She giggles.

                    JACK
          (to himself)
          A-men.

                    CHANTEL
          Hey J.B., how you doin?

> JACK
> Fantastic, you got a twenty-
> forty Hold'em seat?

She turns around and looks at the marker board full of
initials.

> CHANTEL
> No, but you're first up.

She marks his initials. JACK buys a rack of chips. There
is a commotion at a nearby table. A player throws his
cards at the dealer and knocks his chair over. Security
comes. He is ejected roughly, spilling drinks and yelling.
The other players barely notice.

> CHANTEL
> J.B., You want that twenty
> seat?

> JACK
> Christ.

JACK takes the seat. The dealer is straightening the
cards, unaffected. The FLOOR MAN apologizes to her but she
pays no attention. She is looking at JACK.

> FLOOR MAN
> Sorry about that Bren.

The FLOOR MAN leaves. JACK glances at BRENDA. There is an
untouched plate full of chili dogs and French fries on a
mobile tray next to his seat.

ESTABLISH BRENDA: Top section dealer. Blond, pretty,
buxom, but not thin. Her skirt is short and her tuxedo
shirt is unbuttoned suggestively. JACK motions to the
tray.

> JACK
> This for me?

> BRENDA

Sure, you hungry?

JACK looks at the food.

                    JACK
          Famished.

JACK wheels the tray into the aisle, then sits down. The
guy in the seat next to him leans in to talk.

                    PLAYER #1
          You sure you want that seat?

                    JACK
          Pretty sure. Why, did somebody
          just puke on it?

                    PLAYER #1
          Last guy in that seat dropped
          two racks in half an hour.

                    JACK
          Yeah? Well, anybody that eats
          chili dogs at seven o'clock in
          the morning doesn't deserve to
          win.

JACK flags down a cocktail waitress.

                    JACK
          Jack Daniel's.

                    PLAYER #1
          No kidding, the guy never even
          got to eat his breakfast, he lost
          every hand.

                    WAITRESS
          (coyly)
          How do you like it?

                    JACK
          (uncoyly)
          In a glass.

BRENDA is still checking out JACK as the first hand is
dealt. PLAYER #1 is leaning in for recognition.

                    JACK
          Well I've already eaten my
          breakfast, I had cereal. Do
          you know what kind it was?

                  PLAYER #1
          Apple Jacks?

                    JACK
          Close. Lucky Charms. I
          raise.

PLAYER #1 calls. Four other players call. The flop comes
ten, deuce, six, all different suits. JACK checks. PLAYER
#1 bets. Everybody calls. JACK raises.

                   BRENDA
          Raise to forty.

Everybody calls. The turn comes King of the fourth suit.
JACK checks. PLAYER #1 pauses, looks at JACK and bets.
Everybody calls. JACK raises.

                   BRENDA
          Make it eighty.

PLAYER #1 re-raises.

                   BRENDA
          One-twenty.

One other player calls. the rest fold. JACK just calls.

                    JACK
          Put an ace out there.

The river comes queen. JACK acts upset. He motions like
he is going to toss them in the muck pile. He checks by

tapping his cards on the table. PLAYER #1 bets. The other
player folds. JACK brings his cards back and looks at them
again. He raises. PLAYER #1 calls angrily. JACK turns
over ace-jack. The dealer matches up his cards, and pushes
the ten, king, queen up.

> BRENDA
> Ace high straight.

PLAYER #1 is beside himself. BRENDA pushes the pot to
JACK. He tips her two yellow, five dollar chips.

> PLAYER #1
> You check-raised me on the turn
> with a gut shot straight draw?

> JACK
> Did I?

> BRENDA
> Thank you honey.

> JACK
> Thank you. Do it again and
> I'll double it.

BRENDA smiles and deals JACK his second card with extra
emphasis.

FADE TO: The end of the next hand. BRENDA is pushing up
the winning hand of ace-queen. An ace came on the river.

> BRENDA
> Two pair, aces up.

BRENDA pushes the pot to JACK. JACK scoops the chips with
both hands and stacks them.

> PLAYER #1
> God damn it! That seat's been
> ice cold all night. You sit
> down and beat me on the river
> two hands in a row! How'd you
> do that?

> JACK
> I cheat. Just kidding.

JACK tosses four chips to BRENDA. He rolls up his sleeves and winks.

> BRENDA
> Thank you honey.

> JACK
> Do it again and I'll double
> it.

CUT TO: BRENDA's POV: She is staring at JACK's large stacks of chips.

> BRENDA
> I like your necklace.

> JACK
> (to her cleavage)
> I like the way you deal.

JACK's drink comes. He hands the WAITRESS a chip and knocks back his shot.

CUT TO: EXT. JACK and BRENDA skipping arm in arm to the parking lot. They pass an ambulance. JIMMY is being loaded into it. They are oblivious. The JUICE MAN walks up. ROCCO stands beside him. The medics leave. The JUICE MAN looks at ROCCO.

FADE OUT:

FADE IN: INT. JACK and BRENDA are in JACK's dorm. Things are hot and heavy.

CUT TO: JILL and BRUNETTE looking through magazines in JILL's dorm room.

ESTABLISH BRUNETTE: Tall and thin knockout with tons of curly black hair and a supermodel figure.

> BRUNETTE

Are you still going to Vegas for
your birthday?

                    JILL
Yeah, wanna come?

                    BRUNETTE
I can't, I've got rehearsal. Is
Jack gonna be there?

                    JILL
Of course.

                    BRUNETTE
Are you sure? Didn't you have
plans with him last night? What
did you do again? Oh yeah, he
didn't show up. Big surprise.
Didn't he stand you up like
twice last week too?

                    JILL
Yeah but he promised he'd make
it up to me. I think he's
planning something special for
my birthday.

                    BRUNETTE
Really. What makes you think
that?

                    JILL
Well, we're all going to Vegas
right? My brother, Mark, me
and Jack, it's like been
planned, but I think Jack's up
to something because he's not
going with the rest of us. He's
driving by himself.

                    BRUNETTE
He's probably gonna bring a
date.

CUT TO: JACK's room. BRENDA is lying on top of JACK. She
is topless and kissing him.

                    BRENDA
I can't believe you don't have
a girlfriend.

ACKNOWLEDGMENTS

I WOULD LIKE TO TAKE this space to thank no one. I did it all by myself…

JK. ☺

I would like to profusely, deeply, and truly thank the following individuals, without whom this book would never have been written or published:

Munchy, Tricky, Admiral Barney, Dr. Plinky, Tee-ha, KLC, Bonnie Baroo, Skipper Fucking Bob, Kelly Kelly Kelly, Miss Malia, Christmas Carol, Freewheeling Frank, Uncle Tony, Aunt Reen, Uncle Blondie, Gwen Skye, Annie, Allie, Comma Emma, Renny, Rikki Rockett Chopper, Roja, Culvargghhh, Andre, Cuzin Pon Godson Joseph and all the cousins, Mikey The Thumb, T-bone, Roget, Roro, Big E, Char-Char, Crooklyn Jake, Baseball Dave, The Princess of PV, God, all the grandparents, Mona, Babs, J-Fred, Nancy, Beach Angel Angelique, Saint Tom, Aunt Sylvia, Burt the land crab, Lea Thompson, The Loge-monster, PJ Maple, Sass Man, Tom Cat, Sir Gusto, Cuda, Shark, Julie, Pretty Daisy, Mad Margaret, Lord Gabriel, the kid who backed me that one year in the 1k buy-in Limit Hold'em Tournament at the WSOP where I made it to day two and

successfully check-raised Doyle Brunson (won the hand), whose name I never knew, Ventura Bob, J.B., AKA, The Wolf of Wall Street, Jessika, Mia, Rachel, Rhymin' Ryan, Dan the Man, Mr. MacGyver, the Smiths, Papa Vaughn, Marie, Aram Don't Scare'em, Jorge Coppola, Daphna and Jason, Petitioner, David Geffen, Bill Weir, the dealers, floor people, servers, cooks, bartenders, cashiers, security guards, and chip runners at the Normandie and Hollywood Park Casinos, the Eagles, Billy Joel, Seely Dan, the Beatles, the Stones, Elton John, David Bowie, Lou Reed, James McMurtry, Steve Earle, Robert Earl Keen, Tom Petty, Stevie Nicks, Linda Ronstadt, and Jackson Browne.

ABOUT THE AUTHOR

JEFFREY ALLAN GROSSO IS THE author of several scintillating books, screenplays, short stories, feature articles, songs, and poems. He has worked as a copywriter, editor, poker columnist (under the byline "Chip Stax"), and professional poker player. His column, "Chip Stax's Advanced Quantum Theories of Texas Hold'em," ran in *Poker Digest Magazine* for three years and is considered to be the first humor column to focus specifically on Texas Hold'em.

He has also worked as an antique clock dealer, commercial real estate salesman, car salesman, prep cook, line cook, waiter, bartender, wood splitter, and handyman. He currently resides in Redondo Beach, CA where he still plays in a weekly Texas Hold 'em tournament with the world-renowned Euclid Rangers. He continues to hold his own, and a little bit of theirs.